Third Sex Life

by

Vennessa St. John

"I am just me, be yourself..."

\- Vennessa

Foreword

I am not a therapist, nor do I claim to be any kind expert in transgenderism, gender identity, gender roles, etc. All I can do is speak from my own personal experience in hopes that it will help others to understand me and my life a little better. If this in turn helps others to understand themselves or others in the transgender community, even better.

This book is not about preaching or trying to convince anyone of anything. It is not about who is right and who is wrong. It is not about telling others who they should be, how they should act, how they should dress, or how they should describe themselves. This book is simply about how I see the world and how I identify with it through my own personal observations and experiences. This is in no way a guide for others to base their real life decisions on. That being said, please feel free to read on and take a journey inside the life of a model, a musician, an artist, a photographer, a writer, a gear head, a comedian, a composer, a dominatrix, a porn star, a bodyguard, a director, a producer, a business owner, a family member, a computer enthusiast, a clothing designer, a friend and most importantly a human being. There is far more to a person than just their gender or outward appearance.

ONE

Even though this is not really an autobiography I think I will start at the beginning to help give some clarification to those who are concerned with the sexual identity aspect of life, or, of my life anyway. This may help them to see where I am coming from, although it is doubtful anyone will ever see where I am going!

In my earliest childhood memories, from, I'd say, around the ages of four, five and six, I always felt feminine and identified more with the female gender, although not *completely*.

I was never molested, or forced to dress up like a girl or any of that cliché psycho babble which seems to be perpetuated by Hollywood and the porn industry. I had a very normal, childhood. My parents were not abusive or neglectful or dismissive. I never craved my parents' attention due to feelings of being ignored. They read me bedtime stories, tucked me in at night, yelled at me when I did something stupid. I had chores to do, school to go to, etc.

I was very artistic from a very early age, mostly

pencil drawings (we'll get to the obsession with music later!) and fascinated with science and science fiction. I think it was my mother who taught me to read at a very early age. I remember very clearly beginning to read full novels when I was only five years old. The first was Peter Benchley's "JAWS".

We ate dinner as a family, there was no yelling and screaming, my parents weren't drunks or drug addicts. We went to big family cookouts, gatherings, weddings, with all the cousins. We chased fireflies at dusk in the summer, went camping, took family trips to Disney World. There was nothing sinister about my childhood.

One of the most important things I remember about the very early years of my life, something which continues to this day, is that when I dream I am pretty much always female or feminine in my dreams. This is of course when I have a dream that I am actually *in.* I have a lot of cool dreams about situations that I am merely observing like watching a movie.

Anyway, normal childhood. No abandonment issues, no abuse, no neglect, no drugs, no divorced parents. Nothing. Pretty standard and pretty boring. Had both parental role models. No late night sneaky uncle touching me or a nanny forcing me to dress up in little girl clothes. I didn't torture small animals, I didn't fight with other kids at school. I got straight A's in school. Normal, at least

4

for the era I was a kid in. Things seem very different today!

From as far back as I can remember I identified with the female lifestyle more than the male. I didn't want to be the stubbly bearded, rugged hero in the movies or play sports or anything. I always related more to the women. I wanted to dress like them and feel like them. I wanted to be soft and pretty, to smell nice and grow my hair long. I would see the glam pictures of female models in my mother's or sister's magazines and loved the clothes and the make-up. It came very naturally to me to behave like that and want to dress like that, but at a very early age I also learned that doing so was not socially acceptable, especially in a devout Catholic household. Thus I was forced to keep it a secret. For a while at least. It's not much of a secret these days!

I remember how thrilled I was when I found boxes of my older sister's old clothes (a lot were apparently hand-me-downs from relatives) in the attic that had been stored there for whatever reason. Whenever I could get some time alone I would dress up in them, pretty much just the dresses and skirts and blouses with a bra and panties underneath. I was never big on pants, probably because they seemed too masculine and I had to wear them just about all the time anyway.

I was never one of those kids you always hear about who stole their mother's or sister's clothes. I didn't really need to because there always seemed to be boxes of stuff coming and going, plus I wasn't raised that way. Occasionally I would sneak into my mother's room and try things on when she was out (this was later when I was older and she could leave me alone to run to the store or the neighbor's), but that was pretty muchthe extent of it. I pretty much had my own little collection of things with plenty of places to stash them because we lived in one of those big three story colonial farm houses. I'm guessing that's why I'm not afraid of the dark or ghosts. When you grow up in a house that would be a stereotypical Hollywood haunted house today, it kind of desensitizes you!

Dressing up as a girl was not a sexual thrill for me, it just felt natural. To this day if I put on men's clothes, even just shorts or jeans and a T-shirt, I feel like I'm crossdresing or wearing an uncomfortable work uniform that I can't wait to get out of. However the way I dress as a female today is the result of a long journey through style and life that culminated in a combination of look, feel, style and artistic expression. It saddens me a little to think that today people seem to be discouraged from expressing themselves, their individuality, through the way they dress. In the 1980's even thought there were trends and trendy people just like every generation, there was still a lot of emphasis on expressing your personality through your own unique clothing choices. It seems today like there are a limited number of style choices and everyone in each clique wears the same uniform. Like sports teams! Like you have the urban/gangsta baggy pants, big chains, sideways ball cap look, the goth dressed-in-black, dyed black hair with extreme make-up look, the heavy metal jeans and concert shirts look, the 9 to 5'er polo shirt-dress pants-or suit and tie look, etc. In each group they all try to dress the same. I can't even count how many people I've seen with the same tattoos anymore! I remember when only bikers, rockers, and ex-military had tattoos and you rarely ran across two people with the same one unless they were in the same band, biker club or military unit. I'm not by any means knocking people for the way they dress, everyone should be able to do their own thing, but it just seems like people are overly discouraged from doing their own thing. When I was in high school we were bombarded with the whole "be yourself" or "do your own thing" philosophy. It was cool to be different or unique.

Anyway, to return to the topic at hand. As I said before, when I started dressing in girl's clothes it was out of a natural sense that I was female, not some kind of sexual turn on. For some it is a sexual turn on and I am in no way discouraging that. I am simply stating for the psychoanylizers out there who are undoubtedly reading this to prove that I have some easily categorized mental disorder so that they can feel vindicated, that for me it was *not* a sexual thing. I am sure that these same people are also undoubtedly picking apart my writing style, making notes of all my typos, bitching about my run-on sentences, etc. Well guess what? I wasn't an English lit major! I just have a really high IQ (which still can't be accurately measured with any standardized testing) and pretty much everything I do is completely self taught!

I never had a point in my life where I was struggling internally with who I am. I never had that nagging in my mind, "Am I woman trapped in a man's body? Am I gay? Am I sick? Should I stop?" etc. I always felt completely natural being me and being a girl with a penis and testicles. It was *other people* who always seemed to have a problem with it. I was forced to hide it because I did not want to deal with all the taunts and bullshit that come from other's ignorance, especially in the place and era that I grew up in. back then it was far less acceptable or should I say tolerated, than it is today. I still think actual *acceptance* is still a long way off especially when most people (advocates and opposition alike) still talk about tolerance and not just acceptance. I don't know about other people, but I don't want to be *tolerated* for being born the way I am, I would like to be *accepted.* Keep in mind however, I don't *need* or crave acceptance to feel whole or to feel good about myself. I've always been an individual and opposed to what I consider over-conformity. I didn't want to be on the cheer leading squad or run with the "cool" kids or any of that. As far as I am concerned (still to this day) there is nothing "cooler" than being able to think for yourself. I hate peer pressure and always have. I have never succumbed to it either. I never tried drugs or vandalized things or did stupid things just because everyone else was doing it or because I wanted to fit in. I have always just done what I enjoy doing and if nobody else wanted to be in on it then that was their loss. However one thing I have discovered that also seems lost on the generations of today, when you *do* go your own way people who matter seem to respect you more for it and want to join you.

I will delve into the whole style and uniqueness that is me later. For now let's stick to the early years.

I used to love flipping through the fashion magazines and seeing all the really nice outfits that the models wore. They always looked so beautiful and glamorous as opposed to the everyday women I would see around town. Sometimes when we went into the city you would see a lot of women dressed more like the magazine girls but in suburbia not so much. Of course back then pretty much all women wore pantyhose so when I found several pairs that my mother had thrown out because she had gained weight and had to go up a size I was elated.

Luckily, at the time, there was a commercial on TV (they still advertised pantyhose on TV back then!) which showed the proper way to roll on a pair of pantyhose which I am eternally thankful for. There was no one else to teach me how to put them on and I wasn't about to *ask* anyone and not knowing how to put them on can make things very difficult!

Anyway, as soon as I rolled them on and pulled them up to my waist I was hooked. They were so soft and silky and comfortable and they looked and felt great on my legs. My love for wearing pantyhose grew out of my natural tendency to be femme and wear women's clothes and not from a sexual fetish. I have been wearing them ever since and I always sleep in a pair with a silky nightie. With satin sheets it is the most cozy, comfortable, relaxing way to sleep, for me anyway. I also wear them all the time when I am awake. I personally think they add a sense of class to every outfit, on top of looking and feeling sensational. Plus, my legs are one of my best features (I've made a modest living modeling them for quite a few years) and I like to show them off. Also it is said that men who like legs, as opposed to being breast men, are intellectuals and I'd rather attract that sort of attention any day! Any real sexual identification with wearing pantyhose and short dresses/skirts didn't come for me until years after I started wearing them, when I discovered what a huge fetish it was for some people. It ended up just being a very convenient coincidence. I liked wearing them and millions of other people liked seeing me in them!

As for shoes, I didn't get my first pair of heels until a few years later but I would try on my mother's when she was out and I could dress up and move around the house with nobody home. My dad would be at work and my brothers and sister would be doing extracurricular activities so I would often get a few hours alone after school. My mother's shoes were big on me because I was still small at that time and they were pretty bland.

This is not all about clothing though and I don't want people to get the wrong impression and start with the analytical crap about me being a transvestite or crossdresser, etc. However it is common knowledge that clothes and shoes are a big part of most women's lives and, as I touched on before, clothing is a major form of outward expression for people in general. So dressing up as a girl was not only natural for me, but it was fun too, and I still find clothes fun and like designing my own or altering other's designs to fit my unique tastes. I believe this stems more from my creativity than from my sexuality. I like designing in general; cars, guitars, jewelry, clothing.

Getting back to growing up, we moved to Florida

(of all places) when I was about twelve years old and the *real* fun began. Florida in the early 1980's (especially in the tiny back-wood hick town we lived in) was very repressed. The junior high school I went to was segregated (socially if not legally) and built and run like a prison. It was surrounded by high chain link fences with barbed wire on the top and it wasn't even in a bad neighborhood! The gates were left open at night when the school was vacant but locked closed during the day if that tells you anything. All the African-American kids stayed together in their areas and all the redneck kids (rebel flag hats and all) stuck together in their areas with very little intermingling. This however did change drastically by the time I reached my senior year. By the time I was a senior it seemed like everyone hung out with everyone and there was really no fighting. It seemed like the whole 80's/MTV thing really opened people up and actually reduced racial and social tensions. I was finally able to grow my hair long by then too thanks to whole hair band sensation turning everyone "metal". My hair was down to my ass by the time I graduated and everyone (especially the girls) thought it was cool as hell. I had begun learning to play the guitar when I was about seven years old and was immersed in music theory from kindergarten right through college. I even played in the school band in junior high. Having long hair and being able to actually play the guitar in the late 80's was basically like being a superhero!

A few years before moving to Florida I had begun to start having my first interest in sex and found myself relating more to the women in the dirty magazines (found in my brother's/cousin's clubhouses out in the woods) than the men. When I would get aroused I was thinking about being the woman, not the man.

Not long before we moved I had my first sexual experiences with a male friend about the same age as me while perusing the dirty magazines and it felt completely natural to me. I don't however believe or accept that one's *gender identity* is the same as their *sexual orientation* or one dictated by the other. Lesbians are still women and gay men are still men. I will talk more later about my sexual orientation or preference. Right now I am concerned only with laying the ground work to help the reader better understand my views of today.

After moving to Florida the thought of "coming out" or anyone finding out who I really was inside was rather horrifying. The Klan was still very active in the county we lived in if that gives you and idea of the situation. Anyway, I had the typical high school experience; dated girls (not many), went to parties, got into fights. I lifted weights and tried to stay butched up so that I wouldn't get beat up. It turned out I was unnaturally strong for my

13

size (and still am), a genetic trait passed down apparently because my brothers and sister are the same way. So everyone was pretty much afraid to mess with me, plus when I was about twelve martial arts movies were all the rage so me and my friends were always trying to learn "ninja" techniques wherever and whenever we could. This developed into a full blown love of martial arts training (for me at least) and I learned quite a lot by the time I was senior. In fact, by the time I graduated high school I was taking on "black belts" (still not a big fan of Westernized training or the belt system) and winning. Since then I have done years of in depth training but I will touch on that later also. I'm sure there will be critics who want to try challenge the authenticity of my claims but they can lick me. This book is not about what a bad-ass I think I am or claiming any heroic deeds. It's about my perspective on life as a third gender. If any of the critics want to meet with me in private and see my resume I would be more than happy to accommodate (on their dime of course), but that is a separate subject.

Long story short: I spent a few years pretending to be all male and outwardly doing the "male" thing, got sick of living a lie and living my life according to what a bunch of ignorant people around me thought was "normal" and decided that I would only hide just enough to be able to get through the bullshit of everyday life so that I could keep a day job and pay my bills. I went back to being me. It didn't take long for my body to go back to be being femme (in fact no matter how much I worked out I just couldn't bulk up and maintain a "man's body" anyway). I don't really have any body hair (not like a man's anyway) and I don't really grow facial hair (and no I'm not a Native American!). I had been forced to cut my hair short for work but a recession during the Clinton years afforded me the time to grow it back and after that I refused to ever cut it again. Also during this time my mother had passed away and I had sustained some pretty extensive, life threatening injuries which I am not going to get into here. Suffice it to say, I broke a lot of bones and took a few years to heal up.

Ultimately I returned to being femme as full time as possible, putting on the occasional show for society so that they would believe I was "normal" and I wouldn't have to deal with as much ignorance and hate at home as I did out in the rest of the world. I did not, however, lie to the few women I dated or marry someone and keep it a secret. I never duped a man into thinking I was woman either. The few genetic women that I did date actually met me while I was enfemme and were attracted to me that way. When we did break up it was not over my gender identity, but typical relationship things, growing apart, etc.

On the internet I was able to find endless articles,

interviews, etc about everything from transexuality to gender dysphoria, crossdressing, transvestism, being intersexed. I talked with literally thousands of other "Tgs" or "Tgurls" in the chatrooms, most of them talking about their inner struggles with their sexual identities. They talked about hormone therapy and gender reassignment surgery, etc. None of this really seemed to apply to me. I didn't dress for a sexual thrill, I had no desire to re-assign my sex, didn't take hormones, I wasn't a crossdresser (like I said, it's not about the clothes). It seemed to me that I was just about the only one who was happy with who she was. This made me feel sad for all those people who were struggling not only with what society tells them they should be, but with themselves about who *they* think or feel they are.

After reading endless articles on the subject the closest thing I could find to relate to was being intersexed. Psych tests that I took (mostly for work) showed that I use both halves of my brain (creative and analytical – left brain/right brain) which is apparently the rarest type, most people are either left brain or right brain dominant. All of the "are you female or male brained" tests that I took came out female and all of the many, many psychological tests that were required for doing security work came back perfectly normal. In fact I usually had to take them twice because the test takers insisted "no one was *that* normal". This I attribute again to having had a normal, non-abusive, non-neglectful childhood. In this I consider myself very lucky, especially after hearing thousands of horror stories about other people's childhoods!

So I now refer to myself (when I need to refer to myself) as shemale. If this is offensive to anyone too bad. Women are called female, men are called male, I am a third sex which is basically a combination of the two. I am a woman with a predominantly female body who happens to have a penis and testicles. So if there should be some kind of label for my gender, I prefer the term shemale and will continue to refer to myself as such, no matter who it offends. No one has the right to tell me who I am. I am not transitioning from anything to anything, I am not simply crossdressing (I'm still the same person inside even if I am naked). I am not a transvestite because I am not just dressing up in women's clothes for a sexual thrill.

Personally I don't care for all these labels that have been created by the medical profession to describe people of the TG community. Even though I don't consider myself transgender I do consider myself part of the TG community. There is nowhere else that I fit in and isolating ourselves based on small differences is not good. Do we want to end up with *just* the transgender community, *just* the intersexed community, *just* the transvestite community and so on? Isn't there enough confusion already without separating into even more, smaller groups all fighting independent battles? It seems to me that if we stick together and minimized the in-figthing and discrimination within the TG community, we will definitely make more headway along the path to acceptance.

So hopefully now you, the reader, have a better understanding of how I see myself as a person. A better idea of my gender identity and not my *sexual* identity or preference. I did not just wake up one day and decide to put on a dress and run around calling myself a shemale. I truly was born this way and I am perfectly happy being me. It's other people that seem to have a problem with it and the media trying to relate it to them as a "condition" or "illness" does not help. I am not confused, or sick. I am simply a different sex. Are women *tolerated* by men for being female? Are men *tolerated* for being male? No, they are *accepted.* They are simply of different genders. So are we.

TWO

Now that you (hopefully) have a pretty good understanding of who I am, from a gender standpoint at least, I think I can forge on.

Living life as me certainly has it's ups and downs, like anyone's life, but having to deal with the stigma society has placed on being "different" or a member of the TG community is certainly a bigger one of the "downs".

Wouldn't it be nice to be able to go wherever you want, whenever you want without fear of being discriminated against, snickered at, insulted or even beaten and or killed?

The larger portion of my social life revolves around the GLBT (Gay, Lesbian, Bi, Trans) community. The simple fact is that they are the most accepting of who I am. This is not to say that there isn't discrimination within this community because there is. Unfortunately there is far more discrimination within this community than there should be and probably more than the average outsider would believe.

Still it is safer and more comfortable to socialize within the GLBT community (for me at least) than to try to force myself upon the "straight" community and have to deal with the ignorance peppered through out.

That is not to say that the "straight" community is all bigoted and ignorant towards members of the TG community but it is certainly more predominant in my experience.

Plus GLBT bars and clubs are more fun to me. Even if I was genetically all female I would still hang out with the same people in the same places. In all the years that I have been in bars and clubs, from playing music as a "guy" to just hanging out with friends in the gay bars I have only ever seen one fight break out in a gay bar (started by a "straight" guy looking for trouble) and I have lost count of how many I have seen break out in "straight" bars/clubs. Usually more than one a night.

For the most part, I have rarely run into any real trouble, possibly because most people just assume I am female, but I know this is not always the case for many "gurls". I was lucky enough to be born with a very female appearance (if I run to the store in guy's clothes I still get ma'ammed and called her or she which I secretly take as a huge compliment), but I know not everyone is so lucky.

Occasionally when I am out some inconsiderate asshole will notice something that clues them in that I might not be all female and will make a comment or snide remark. Sometimes I will reply with something like, "Is it really worth getting your ass beat over?". I still have a hard streak from years of being a bodyguard and I am confident in my fighting ability. I also carry a gun. I worry less about survival than I do about the media and legal backlash following defending myself.

I have also found through years of experience that there are not many entirely "straight" men around. I like to say, "There is no such thing as a straight guy when his friends aren't around!". It's been my experience that the guys who know so much about TGs don't just know through idle curiosity, looking up stuff on the internet. They know because on some level it excites them. There are also a lot of dangerous individuals out there who are confused about their own sexual identity or at odds in some way with themselves and go out picking up TGs to have sex with them, then freak out, often getting violent afterward. When they realize what they have done, they become disgusted with themselves and take it out on the gurl. I learned early on to identify and avoid these types of men, usually through their body language, attitude, speech, etc. In many ways these individuals are far more dangerous than the average hater on the street, but in many instances they are one and the same.

In general though, I have rarely had a problem when it comes to shopping, getting gas, things like that. Usually when shopping for clothes the store associates are very nice and helpful. Of course I avoid shopping in places like the larger mega market stores which are havens for mobs of ignorant lowlifes. The smaller boutique type stores, outlet stores, department stores etc are better and you are less likely to run into troublemakers. Again this really has nothing to do with gender identity because I avoid these people regardless. I don't know too much about the situation around the rest of the nation, but where I currently live it seems everywhere you go people are looking to cause trouble. I see fights all the time that have nothing to do with me. It seems like everyone around here drives that way too. Way too much road rage.

Which brings me to a good point. TG life and the fight for acceptance is hard enough when you are dealing with just everyday "normal" people. It's even harder when it seems like everyone, everywhere is just looking for an excuse to fight or cause trouble.

I try to just go about my life and stay away from conflicts these days. For years I was paid to deal with it on a daily basis and it never really bothered me. It was just a job. Some scumbag could scream a me and call me all kinds of names because I was having his ass arrested for something stupid he did and it was nothing. It wasn't personal. I would never give it a second thought or let it keep me up at night. But when I'm not getting paid to deal with it I am not going to go out of my way to get involved. That's what the police and security guards get paid for.

However when it *is* personally directed at me that is a different story. I don't put up with that crap from anybody. I know how to de-escalate a situation though so I try my best to do so, but I stand up for myself.

Getting back to the GLBT community, as I said, it has it's fare share of discrimination. It has been my experience that within the "T" part of the community there is way too much discrimination and in-fighting. There seems to be all these little cliques of gurls who hate other gurls for dressing too slutty (in their opinion), gurls who hate gurls because they get implants, gurls who hate gurls because they are "just crossdressers or transvestites", etc. My problem has always been that I just don't fit in with any of them really. I try to get along with all of them but many are way too hung up on the categorizing. So many of them run around preaching acceptance and tolerance then they turn around and bash each other and separate into little sub-groups. They even discriminate based on income!

This whole in-fighting situation just adds more difficulty in the fight for acceptance. It's hard enough fighting to be accepted by society without fighting to be accepted by your own people.

Things would probably go a lot smoother if we could all get along and maintain a unified front. That is not to say that everyone should conform to one ideal and or image, but that everyone in the community should at least work toward accepting each other and not bicker and nit pick about the little differences. Again, isn't that the point? We want to be accepted regardless of our differences to mainstream society, so, how then can we have that expectation of others while discriminating within our own groups over what we perceive as differences?

I myself have avoided joining or dropped out of many online groups and social networks after being exposed to their endless rules and expectations. Rarely has anyone every attacked me directly, but their statements to others about how they should dress, or behave just seemed far too hypocritical for me to join or remain affiliated with the groups. As I mentioned before, it is not about how you dress or behave, nor is it about your sexual orientation, it is about who you are inside as a person. A genetic woman is still a woman no matter how she is dress. In an equal world or a world where transgenderism or a third sex is accepted the same thinking should apply. A transsexual or intersexed person is still the same person inside regardless of their outward appearance.

Indeed there are clothing fetishists and people

who dress as the opposite gender simply for the sexual thrill of it, but there are also genetic women who like fetish wear or wearing slutty outfits for a sexual thrill. There are also genetic women who like to dress sexy, with some class, because they are proud of their bodies and the work they put into looking good. Looking and feeling sexy makes you feel good about yourself and regardless of what you may have heard or read, there is nothing wrong with it. Didn't the Supreme Court rule years ago that raping a woman simply because for the way she was dressed was not justified? So if *real* women can wear sexy clothes in public and deep down inside you feel that you are a *real* woman, shouldn't you be allowed to dress and behave like a *real* woman. I don't criticize people for doing their own thing or dressing how they want to dress, but *all* people should be treated equally when it comes to this. If an outfit just isn't working or conveying the image you want it too it's probably just not the right outfit for the situation regardless of your gender. It's up to the individual to take control and determine what personal image they want to convey. It is not up to the rest of us to act as the Fashion Nazis and complain that the clothing choices of a few of us is a reflection on the entire gender. A genetic woman wearing an outfit that other women don't like is not a reflection on the entire female gender around the world. It is a reflection on her personally. This is why it upsets me when I read posts online or hear other TGs saying that "bad crossdressers" or transvestites posting pictures or going out in slutty, trashy outfits hurts us all. It shouldn't hurt us or our fight for equality anymore than Miley Cyrus' antics hurt the entire female gender!

I have seen hundreds of posts and comments online trashing gurls over their physical appearance. This is just appalling. Not everyone can be a super model. Not everyone has the money or opportunity to be perfect. I see genetic women of all shapes and sizes everyday and it is wrong for the elitists of the TG community to demand that every TG person be a perfect, flawless sculpture.

Also, surgery is not for everyone. Many are happy just being themselves and don't feel the need to alter their physical appearance, nor should they be badgered into it just to put other's at ease. That just leads right back to what I said before about hypocrisy. You shouldn't run around preaching that everyone should accept you for who you are, then refuse to accept others for who they are. It is a two way street, a double edged sword and a broad, sweeping plane of diversity.

I have personally seen little cliques of gurls out in clubs gang up on and ridicule fledgling crossdressers and transsexuals who were merely trying to find and express themselves with no one to guide them. This behavior is beyond reprehensible and if I witness it I will *never* socialize with those kind of people ever again. They are nothing more than bullies trying to feel better about their own shortcomings by bringing someone else down. I always try to help out girls who are new to being themselves and give them encouragement. With no one to guide you it can be very difficult to negotiate the world of womanhood as far as clothing choices, make-up, social graces etc. Remember, most genetic girls have mothers, sisters, or girlfriends to teach them and give them pointers when they are growing up. Many transgender girls are closeted and don't get that opportunity. I myself learned how to do my make-up from a book on modeling that my sister had. I don't remember the name of the book but it went into explicit detail about how make-up is done on professional models for film and photo shoots, explaining everything from foundation to eyes, to facial structure highlighting.

The overall point I am trying to make here though is that regardless of your gender identity you should be able to be yourself, be proud of who you are as person, receive support and acceptance from your own peer group and ultimately be accepted by society.

No one should have to be self conscious about *who* they are. Everyone should be able to just be themselves and deal with all the same everyday problems on an even playing field; paying the bills, getting to work on time, paying your taxes, etc. Not worrying about getting arrested for having to use the wrong restroom or getting beaten up or even killed because of what might or might not be between your legs.

I didn't want to get too preachy or go on a rant but I think the whole thing about working together and accepting each other is very important. Now that that is out of the way I will move on to lighter subjects!

Since I have (hopefully) instilled in the reader that this book is about being fully accepted as a third gender and not about fetishism and sexuality linked directly to transgenderism or crossdressing, from here on out everything should be regarded as pertaining to the *person* and not the *gender.* For instance when I talk about clothing or fetish wear or sexual orientation it should mean the same as if they were the personal preferences of a genetic female woman.

As I said before, I have my own style and I like to look good when I go out. I like to look and feel sexy and I like to show off my attributes a little. I do *not* however gout wearing the wrong size clothing or with my genitals wagging in the wind. I am not knocking people who do this, I am simply saying I don't do it myself. I have seen just as many "real" woman out in public showing too much as I have seen crossdressers and yes, even transsexuals, so be careful where you point fingers and who you say isn't dressing or acting like a "real" girl. Remember, the majority of prostitutes are "real" women!

Anyway, my own personal style is a culmination of being a child of the 80's and being a rocker/metal chick at heart. I like wearing short, tight dresses, stiletto heels, spikes, chains, skulls, etc. Like I mentioned earlier I always wear pantyhose. I believe they lend a certain air of class to a short dress, and as I said before, my legs are one of my best features so I like to show them off a little. I'm sure some day I'm going to be too old to work the leg angle so I'm going to get all the mileage I can out of them while I'm still young enough!

I'm not a nine to fiver, overly conservative type so I don't pretend to be or dress like one. I have nothing against people who dress conservatively, it's just not my thing and I am going to do my own thing. I also like expressing myself through my clothing. I am artistic and creative and I enjoy designing my own clothes when I can. I have an affection for bolero jackets, probably due in part to keeping my butt and abs in shape and not wanting to cove them up. Unlike a lot of women I am not self conscious about my body, but I'm not a creepy exhibitionist either. I'm not one of those people who run around getting a thrill out of almost getting caught with my junk hanging out or giving people up-skirt glimpses.

I've never been big on the casual look. I save that for around the house, doing yard work, etc. When I go out in public I try to look my best simply because that's the way I was raised. Comb your hair, stand up straight, tuck in your shirt, that kind of thing. I'm not an obsessive compulsive but I do like to stay clean and well groomed.

There can be a fine line between classy and slutty and it takes a certain finesse to negotiate it. Again, I am not preaching, merely offering advice. The secret I have found for looking good is finding what kind of clothes flatter your particular build or shape and buying clothes that are the right size. To look good (no matter what gender you are), you should play to your strengths. For instance, in my case I accentuate my legs, eyes, butt, tummy and lips. If I had big breasts I would accentuate the cleavage. I know many girls (real or transgender) see things in ads, on models, etc., fall in love with the outfit and are hell bent on making it work for them. The sad fact is that regardless of what Hollywood tells us, this is not the case. I have seen literally hundreds of outfits that I just adored but they are designed for tiny, curvy little women, not a five foot ten inch, toned, aging porn star. So I do not try to wear them in public. Experiment, find out what works and plan accordingly. Also keep in mind that the outfits in the ads are custom tailored to fit the models in the ads and a lot of them end up not looking good on *anyone* else.

Where you are going may also dictate what you wear, at least for me it does. I usually don't go out much except to hang out with friends at the clubs on weekends. During the week I am usually home sulking in poverty and wishing it was Friday night. So when I do go out I am usually dressed for clubbing. It's fun to flirt with and tease the guys even if you are not out looking for sex, but you still have to know what you are doing, who you are dealing with and be aware of your surroundings. I have a lot of experience dealing with people in clubs so I know who to avoid and who I can have harmless fun with, plus most people know me at the places I go to.

It can be very dangerous for the club-novice TG to go out, even to a GLBT club. As I mentioned before, there are still a lot of dangerous people out there and not just homophobic closet cases, but really dangerous people, even serial killers.

Some years ago I was at a club in Clearwater, Florida called Z109 (long since gone and bulldozed) hanging out with the local TG club crowd and some guys. I go out and come home alone most of the time. I do not recommend this to other TGs or genetic women. I have pretty extensive self defense/martial arts training and as I said before, I carry a gun and know how to use it. Anyway, the next day I saw on the news that one of the TG girls that we all knew, whom I had talked to just before she left the club, had been stabbed to death by a man that had flirted with me earlier that night and hinted about me going home with him. It seems in our world it is always just right around the corner.

That was not the only incident I had experience with at that particular club, although it was the worst. Many nights when entering or leaving the club, the overflow of late night neighborhood scumbags from the convenience store next door would generate trouble.

On one night in particular there was some sort of scuffle right outside the front door when a "straight" guy attacked a couple of drag queens then sped off. No one was seriously hurt that I know of. I had been inside when it happened and we all came running outside to see the car speed away as one of the drag queens was trying to put her wig back on.

In that same parking lot I was approached more than once by guys either asking the typical mundane questions of ignorance; "Are you a guy? Do you have a dick?" etc, or prattling on about how they didn't judge and what I "was doing" didn't bother them.

These kinds of things make me wonder if these same guys are just as rude to genetic female women in public. Most women I know would smack the crap out of a guy if he talked to them like that. Try going up to a "real" girl in a bar and asking her what's in her pants, if she's a "dike", or if she's really a man. Chances are you will get your ass kicked or at least escorted from the premises!

As far as places to go, again I remind the reader that I am talking about my own personal experiences and most transgender women I presume are more concerned with going to regular places. Also many people in general aren't into the club scene at all. Since transgender women are really just women at heart I'm sure many spend their time going to regular "straight" bars or clubs, restaurants, etc. I personally know several who never set foot in a gay bar. I like going to a few "straight" clubs and places myself, but like I said before I prefer the GLBT clubs because the atmosphere is better.

One place I like is a big goth club that is just for everybody. It's not gay or straight, it's just a club and I have never had a problem there. The people are pretty indifferent to gender in general and its a great place for the "self expressive" crowd to hang out. One of the things I like about it is the gender neutral restroom so one can pee no matter how one is perceived. How great would it be if the rest of the country followed this example?

The main reason I like this club is that my style fits in fairly well there. I don't really feel like I'm among my crowd at say, a country bar. I like the heavy metal/goth crowd that this place draws and it affords me the opportunity to socialize with people who have the same likes or dislikes beyond gender identity. The truth is I spend very little time talking about or consciously thinking about my gender. It only ever comes up when someone else brings it up. In fact it is making writing this book extremely difficult! I have to rack my brain to remember all this!

I used to get bombarded with questions (mostly from women, the guys are usually too embarrassed) when I went out to a lot of the different gay clubs back in the day, but that has really died off. I'm hoping this is due to heightened awareness and progress. They would ask me all the standard questions; "Are you transsexual or a transvestite? Are you a hermaphrodite? Do you still have your dick? Are you taking hormones? Are you going to get surgery?" Luckily for me though, most people don't even realize I'm not just a regular woman even after talking to me for an hour. I get hit on and checked out a lot by lesbians too. The gay men generally aren't interested. They are gay and are attracted to masculinity so the female form doesn't do much for them.

But getting back to style and taste, I love fashion. I love black leather, leather look fabric, spandex, fetish wear, straps, chains. All the heavy metal, rock n' roll and Gothic stuff. I love hard rock and heavy metal music and the whole metal scene so that influences my style. I have a metal/dance album out now that I composed, produced and recorded entirely by myself and promote it as much as possible in the mainstream. I was very surprised at the acceptance and rave reviews of it even though it is openly advertised that I am a TG artist. I expected to get a complete stonewall reaction to it when I first started promoting the music but I am continually getting new fans on Reverbnation and great compliments not only on the music but on my appearance, sexiness, and perseverance. I have not had a single negative remark out of thousands about being TG.

I love music and I would love nothing more than to be successful and tour with a full band playing the same venues as everyone else, but I have met with total resistance locally when it came to putting a band together. I spent several years advertising in the local music scene trying to put a band together and receive not one single response. Any ads that I posted in the same places advertising the same thing but with a *male* persona were flooded with responses. I guess the open minded musicians in Florida just aren't as open minded as they all rave about!

This is the kind of unfortunate ignorance that causes such hardships for TGs in the everyday world. Even major record labels have shown no interest in me or my music even though the general public seems to love it. I even tried an experiment where I set up a profile with the same quality of music under a *male* image and was officially solicited *twice* by a major label that shall remain nameless, with only about *one tenth* of the following!

While this by no means proves discrimination in the music or entertainment industry it certainly suggests it. To me at least.

THREE

It seems to me that some people think gender identity should correspond to personal habits, goals, preferences, etc. I do not believe this to be true. If you are a woman at heart you should only wear frilly girly clothing and do girly things? That's beyond ridiculous. How many genetic females join the military, become fire fighters, police officers, federal agents, etc? Quite many and it does not make them any less female. Why can't a woman be an engineer, a mechanic, a rock star or anything else she wants to be? It is perfectly acceptable (for the most part, women still have their battles to fight for equality as well) for women to take on these formerly "male only" careers.

Who says just because you are a woman you have to like pink, hate sports and act all weak and girly? Certainly not a woman! I have actually heard members of the TG community spout off about how others in the community were a disgrace because they didn't engage in menial "girly"

37

activities. I for one don't like pink and love muscle cars. I love restoring and working on them (although I hate getting all greasy but it comes with the turf) and I love driving them. If I had the money I think I would open my own garage to restore and work on classic muscle cars. The only time anyone would probably ever hear from me would be at car shows or races!

For the most part I am a very strong and independent person but it also doesn't take too much to make me cry and I love cute little stuffed animals. Just because someone is transgendered doesn't mean they have to live up to some bogus social guideline that says they have to do *only* things that society deems feminine. That kind of thinking is ridiculous and sets the whole feminist movement back about fifty years.

That being said, there is the serious issue of outward appearance as it relates to one's own self identification and how this affects the transgender community when it comes to the struggle for equal rights. In other words the ongoing threat of hate and violence against members of the TG community based on our outward appearance and who is *actually* included in the TG community (the "T" in GLBT) based on how they perceive themselves inside.

I'm sure as most members of the TG community are aware, there is currently a heated debate going on over statements made by a famous drag performer (who shall remain nameless here) apparently bashing transsexuals. All of what I am delving into here goes back to the whole philosophy that we need to end the in-fighting and work together toward a common goal – we need equal rights and acceptance for everyone who falls under the umbrella of the TG community.

There are arguments from all sides and from all the different walks of TG life about who is encompassed by this umbrella and who is not. It has been argued by some that drag queens are not actually members of the TG community because they are simply gay men dressed as women solely for entertainment purposes, i.e, drag is "performance art" and not a TG lifestyle and that many drag performers self identify as male in every day life when they are out of drag. I have seen this to be the case quite often, but, I also know many drag queens that are also transsexuals and live as women when they are not doing shows. The problem seems to come when gay men who identify as male dress up in drag for entertainment purposes and make derogatory remarks (especially publicly with a huge platform like television or the internet) about "trannies".

It has been said that, to the average lay person who is not educated about TG life, these gay male performers appear to be active members of the TG community and fall under the umbrella. This in turn could lead the general public to believe that the remarks, thoughts or opinions of these drag performers represent the entire TG community. Furthermore it is a major concern that public warring between perceived members of the TG community cause great damage to the advancement toward equality. When the general public sees what they are led to believe is a transsexual behaving in such a matter it hurts us all.

Another aspect as I touched on earlier is *who* is actually a member of the TG community and *who* has the right to determine this? This is where things get really touchy. Should drag performers, crossdressers, transvestites, effeminate gay men and masculine lesbians all be included? I have seen it pointed out that many of these people can be perceived by the general public as not meeting traditional gender roles and fall victim to hate generated by that perception. This leads some to argue that this gives them the right to say whatever they want about TG rights and the TG community.

So, then, where is the line drawn, who draws it, and should it be drawn? Who is to start saying who qualifies as a member of the TG community and who doesn't? This makes things very complicated very fast. It makes it difficult to push for equality when presenting to the general public and lawmakers, who expect a clear definition of what the TG community is, before moving forward with rights issues. How do you give trans-women the right to use the women's room or be treated women without giving the same right to "straight" sex offenders and perverts who dress up in women's clothes an peep through windows? It quickly turns into a complicated issue and can spiral out of control into segregation within the community. Are we going to start saying certain people are not trans *enough* because they are not taking hormone replacement therapy or because they haven't had gender reassignment surgery? There are many who can't or don't feel they need to take hormones or have surgery even though they are completely female inside. There are also many who have the outward physical appearance of the opposite gender, the mind of the opposite gender, but with different genitalia who do not want or feel the need to change (much like me).

It is a very complicated issue and there is not going to be any quick fix. However, it seems to me that if a person has sex reassignment surgery that they are then *actually* that sex both physically and psychologically and should therefore be addressed as and treated as such by the law and by society. If a TG goes through therapy, GRS and becomes fully the opposite gender then he or she should be legally regarded as that gender. There should be no legal difference between them and anyone who was born into their true gender identity.

Unfortunately, as I have mentioned, this is still only one aspect of a broad sweeping issue. This still leaves people of mixed gender (intersexed), people who are still transitioning, crossdressers, etc. I should think that logic and reason would dictate that if someone is in transition and has already made the decision to live as their true gender (whether they are planning on GRS or not) then they too should be legally and socially accepted as that gender and not have to wait until they are fully through transition.

Now, this is fine for people who are *transitioning* . What about those of us who aren't? There are still many aspects to the "T" group under the umbrella of the "T" in GLBT. One of them is people like me. We are not all the same so I can only speak from my point of view of who I am. There are those of us who are basically female with male genitalia who are completely female inside and display a naturally female or mostly female outer persona and live as female. What about us? Everyone in the TG community is running around screaming about equality and that the should have the right to be treated as equals and not be forced to be something they are not. So why should people like me be forced to be something we are not? This is what I call the third sex and I am more than happy to include everyone into this group who has not gone through total gender reassignment or has not made the decision to. I don't like to discriminate even though many transsexuals refuse to include me in their definition of "TG".

I don't believe that intersexed people should be bullied by the transgender community into getting GRS or getting out. You want to be who you truly feel you are inside and feel you have that right, then people like us should have that same right. I identify as female even though I have male genitalia. My mind is female and I dress as a female and my appearance is female but I have no thoughts whatsoever about having GRS. I am not a crossdresser or transvestite. I am not an effeminate gay man. As I have said before, the best way I can define myself (besides intersexed) is as a shemale. I should have just as much right as anyone to be myself and live as myself. I was born this way and I like who I am. It seems to me though that I am a minority within a minority. I rarely run into anyone who feels the same way I do about who they are and I have trouble relating to many other members of the TG community. This has caused social problems for me. I have been shunned (so to speak) by most of the local little cliques such as transsexual and crossdresser groups. I am a very open minded and outgoing person and try to be friendly with everyone but as I have mentioned many times, there is still blatant discrimination within the TG community.

It has been my experience that most of the transsexual groups like to get together and talk about their hormone replacement therapy and

43

GRS, neither of which really applies to me, so I get the cold shoulder. I'm hoping it is not like this everywhere, however it has been my experience in the area where I have lived most of my life.

Because I have no plans for GRS and don't really need hormone therapy and because I am and always have been happy with who I am, I have been treated by many transsexuals like I don't belong. When they get talking about hormones and GRS, etc., I often feel a little out of place, I imagine the way a genetic woman probably feels in the same situation.

On the other hand, when the issues of equality and acceptance come up, I can relate. I have the same issues and problems with society that a TG in transition has. Such as the whole restroom issue. I have to be careful where I go to the restroom in public just like them. For all intents and purposes I am physically and mentally the same as a person in mid transition.

I have become quite adept at negotiating the public restroom problem, at least in the area where I live. There are many gas stations in the area that have gender neutral, single restrooms. The one-room kind with one toilet and sink, the locking door and the male and female carton characters on the sign. Also here I am allowed to use the ladies room in the gay bars, although using the men's rooms in them is also socially acceptable. The problem comes when you are out with friends and stop at some random restaurant or you want to go to a "straight" bar/club and they have the large men's restrooms. In many places you can be arrested for using the ladies' room if your driver's license says "male" on it, or beaten and killed for using the men's room, just because.

What I usually do is try to find a gas station with the gender neutral restrooms if I have to go when I am out, or pop into one of the gay bars. I don't drink and generally I try not to have to go to the restroom when I am out period because even if I was one sex or the other I wouldn't want to use most public restrooms around here.

For the most part though, people won't mess with me in public places around here. People around here don't want trouble in their establishments no matter what it's about and there is an almost overbearing police presence here. If you start trouble with anyone the police are going to show up and arrest you regardless. It's the dark parking lots and secluded areas you have to watch out for. Personally I avoid these places and situations out of a general awareness through my training, not because of any gender issues. I can take care of myself and an unsafe area is unsafe no matter what your gender is.

FOUR

Safety is one of the big issues in the TG community and, being that I have years of professional training and experience in this field, as well as being a member of the TG community, I feel that it is somewhat my responsibility to do what I can to help.

Not going out a lone (if possible) is a big help. I know this may not even be an option for many TG people because it can be difficult to make friends. Depending on the area you live in it may not be too much of an issue as far as daytime trips to the supermarket or convenience store. However, many TG people are into the night life, clubbing, etc. This can be dangerous for anyone but especially for TG people when there is so much hate out there.

It would be nice in a utopian society where we could all go where we want and do what we want without fear of persecution or violence, but alas that is not the case. In this post-9-11 world it seems violence has escalated greatly. The internet is overrun with videos of fights,killings, beatings, etc in public places. Some motivated by hate (against gender or race) some just random acts of violence. In today's society it pays to be prepared regardless of your gender or race.

Being by yourself can make you an appealing target for people looking to do harm to others, especially out of hate. Going out with even just one other person can be enough of a deterrent sometimes to keep attackers at bay.

I have found that going to GLBT clubs is generally not an issue. Once you are inside anyway. You may have problems with gaybashers while crossing the parking lot to and from your vehicle. If the establishment is concerned about their patrons and regularly calls the police when troublemakers show up outside this greatly reduces the issue. They will generally get the point and stay away. Also most places I regularly go to will have someone walk you to your car if you request it.

Regular, everyday, "straight" clubs can be a whole different issue. Depending on the area and the management's attitude toward members of the TG community you may be taking a big chance. If we had protection under the law everywhere this would be less of an issue although people are still going to hate us no matter what the law says.

I know many transsexuals in this area who regularly go all the places other people go with little to no trouble. It has been my experience that the more you look like a genetic female the less you are going to be hassled. I have seen posts on the internet from crossdressers who try to go to "straight" bars or restaurants looking obviously like men in women's clothing, who complain about being treated badly. While it is wrong to treat anyone like that it is still a cold hard fact of life that people are going to do it. There are many transsexuals who cannot "pass" in public and this should not automatically give people the right to mistreat them.

The sad fact of the matter, though, is that no matter what laws are passed, certain people will always be a threat to anyone who (to them at least) is easily identifiable as TG. This is where self-defense classes/training come in handy. If at all possible, I recommend to everyone in the TG community to take some kind of self defense courses or training.

I am by no means saying anyone should run out and get into fights, but being able to effectively defend yourself from a physical attack is pretty much a requirement for everyone these days. Prevention is far better though. If you can keep the situation from escalating or arising in the first place you are that much better off. Being aware of your surroundings is a good start. Avoiding bad neighborhoods, dark parking lots/alleys, suspicious looking gangs of people, etc.

I personally carry a gun as well as having

defensive training, but I have also managed to go twenty-plus years without serious incident, simply through knowing how to handle myself in a bad situation.

It truly is too bad that such an emphasis is placed on appearance in our country today. There is also a certain degree of hypocrisy when it comes to discrimination based on appearance. It is not socially acceptable (and as far as I know it is illegal) to discriminate against someone because of their skin color. It seems quite common, however, that people are discriminated against because of their physical appearance, especially when it comes to the TG world. I have personally witnessed TG people being harassed and insulted because they looked masculine. I have even seen videos online of TG people being assaulted and beaten because they appeared to be transgendered. Now if someone were to do this to, say, an African American person, it would be considered a hate crime. You cannot discriminate against someone because of their skin color so why is discrimination based on other physical attributes tolerated in this country? I see people with tattoos discriminated against all the time. Whether it is naturally occurring or not, is this not coloration of the skin? What if someone happened to born spotted or striped like a leopard or tiger? It would not be acceptable to discriminate against them would it? One could then argue that tattoos are elective and not naturally occurring so there is a difference. Yet it is not acceptable to discriminate against genetic females who have breast augmentation even though that is elective and not naturally occurring. So, by that reasoning, shouldn't it be wrong to discriminate against a TG person for having the same surgery? It should definitely be unacceptable to discriminate against TG persons with *naturally* occurring female breasts. Certainly no one should ever have to worry about being assaulted simply because another person doesn't like the way they *look*. So why do the same people who would never tolerate a genetic woman being beaten up for the way she looks seem to tolerate it and sometimes even *condone* it when a TG is beaten up for the same reason. Changing laws will only do so much. People's *attitudes* and *perceptions* need to change as well.

I think true equality for *everyone* would be much more attainable if there was less emphasis on keeping us all separated from each other. A good example of this is, once again, the public restroom issue. I know there is continual bitching about the cost of implementing three gender or gender neutral restrooms in public places, but there are many ways this can be achieved without no real cost.

I have been in many public restrooms that have lines of stalls with individual locking doors on each stall. So why not take existing restrooms like these and designate them gender neutral? Perhaps pass a federal law that requires public places that have multi-stall restrooms already in place to make sure the locks on the individual doors are maintained and that no one can peek in through cracks in the stalls? Other places, like the gas stations and convenience stores I mentioned earlier, already have single person restrooms. Make it a requirement that these are gender neutral. If only one person at a time can use the restroom why would you need to designate it male or female? I've never been in anyone's house that didn't have shared bathrooms and when they have a party men and women take turns using the same restrooms.

I'm sure the issue of men standing at the urinals would come up and people would say that women won't want o use a restroom where they have to walk by a row of men standing at urinals to got tot he bathroom. Simple. Either give the urinals their own stalls with doors (with a stencil or sign with a picture of a urinal on it) or take them out completely. Again, I have never been in a private residence with a urinal. Plus, men, when you are standing at the urinal how do you know who is standing next to you? If "straight" men are getting so uptight about TG people using the restroom why are they *not* getting uptight about gay men using the same restroom? The man standing next to you could be a serial killer, a gay man, a child molester, a male rapist, anything. I personally don't understand why "straight" men would even *want* to use a urinal in the first place.

By keeping the individual stalls already in place and by removing or closing in the urinals you solve all the problems all the way around. Basically you are creating individual restrooms that *anyone* can use and effectively removing the gender issue at little cost and, in the cases of some restrooms I have been in, no cost.

Some may argue that you still have multiple genders mixing in the same room and making people uncomfortable, especially women having to walk by the men, etc. Well what is the difference between that and walking by people in a restaurant, bar or store to use the restroom? You shouldn't be doing anything in the common area of the restroom that you can't do anywhere in public. If you don't have room to do it in a bathroom stall then you probably shouldn't be doing it. As far as the sinks and mirrors are concerned, there is no real need for individual privacy when you are outside the stalls.

Until this issue with the restrooms is resolved we are still faced with the dilemmas of what to do now. As things stand now there are many places where TG people are not allowed to use public restrooms. Seems to me this problem was faced by some other people some years back and the

Federal government stepped in and stopped it. Weren't businesses all over the country also forced by Federal mandate to make all restrooms handicapped accessible?

Getting back on track, I have seen many stories in the press where genetic women have complained about having to share public restrooms with TG people. Apparently the big complaint is that they don't want some pervert who is sexually attracted to women being in the same restroom as them.

What about lesbians? Back to the point I made earlier with the "straight" men in the restrooms. How do these same women know that they're not in the restrooms with lesbians who might be "ogling" their goodies? Hypocrisy again. Should they be allowed to post "no lesbians allowed" signs on their restrooms? Great plan. So how would they know when a lesbian uses the restroom? Because you can spot a lesbian or a gay man quite easily right? Completely wrong.

This brings me back to a point I touched on earlier. Appearance. I have used countless restrooms alongside genetic women who had no clue that I wasn't one of them. Pretty much *every* time I go out in public I end up in conversations with people who have no idea at all that I am not an everyday genetic female. It has also been my personal experience that when I let "straight" people that I am engaged in conversations with know who I am they react differently than they would to someone who looks more masculine. One of the most common responses, especially from the men, is, "Wow, I never would've guessed. You look so good (or so real). It's not my thing but whatever..." and they are usually very polite and can't stop saying "wow". *Then* I often get to hear the other shoe drop and the truth comes out when they follow up with, "You look really good (or really real or something similar)...*not like some you see that look like big ugly guys in dresses.*"

It's like being undercover. They seem to think that because I look really feminine it's OK, but someone who might not look as female as me is some sort of freak or disgrace. Often these same people reveal much about their views on the whole TG issue and it is not pretty.

Firstly they usually make the mistake of thinking that I am going to sympathize with them and come back with some ignorant remark like, " I hear ya! What freaks!" I don't. I usually get a little sadistic, like a cat playing with a mouse, and toy with their heads a little, coming back with things like, "Oh, so you're saying it *wouldn't* be OK for me to be me if I was ugly or more masculine, but it *is* OK because I look like a *real* woman?" By the time I am done with them they are usually tripping all over themselves and apologizing.

The *second* thing I find is how much they actually believe that being TG (or intersexed) is some kind of lifestyle or fashion choice. To which

I generally reply that, "This is me. This is who I am. It's not a fetish or a hobby."

All this stems from ignorance and most people can hardly be blamed for not understanding it. They grew up with no real education about it except Hollywood's sensationalization and demeaning of it and internet porn.

I have met many, many people who were completely ignorant of the entire TG world but were not bad or hateful people and it is wrong to get offended when these people don't know how to talk to you. I have seen many TG's get all in a huff and storm away from people in bars/clubs, etc., bitching about how offended they were that these individuals referred to them as "he" or were "clueless". I have then engaged these (usually completely baffled) individuals in conversation and found them to be very nice, very open minded people who meant no offense at all. They just had never been properly educated in the etiquette involved with talking to TG people. They are like people in a foreign country who do not speak the language. It is not their fault that they don't understand.

Many of them are just curious in the same way anyone would be curious about a visitor from another country. Getting immediately offended by them and storming off is not the answer. Whenever I encounter these people I do my best to answer their questions and help inform them so that they *will* understand and they are generally very open and accepting. When you have a regular conversation with them and they find out you are a regular person just like them, the barriers tend to come down.

Granted this is *not* the case with everyone. There are still plenty of hateful people out there who are going to hate us no matter what, but those people are looking for excuses to hate and be violent. They may preach that they were just raised differently and don't agree with our "lifestyle" as they often refer to it, but that is just a load of crap. When something isn't your "thing" you don't attack it and protest it. You just go your way and leave it alone. I don't like certain kinds of automobiles. I don't get all worked up and protest their existence. I just don't drive them. I don't like certain kinds of food. I don't go into restaurants and make a scene or attack the waiter because those foods are on the menu.

When you start to really think about the behavior of "haters" it becomes evident that there is more to it than just being "raised differently". In most cases there is something *really* wrong there. If they don't attack and hate you they will find someone or something else to attack and hate.

Going head to head with these "haters" may not be the best course of action. I don't know for sure, but I think that maybe if we marginalize them or ignore them a bit and concentrate on educating the people who are ignorant of us but still good natured, we can affect changes that the "haters" will have no choice but to follow. No one wants to be the odd man out or the lone asshole who hates everything and no one agrees with him. Especially int his country today. Focus on educating the majority of the non-haters and the "haters" will be forced to go along.

FIVE

Public image. Or, rather, the public's perception of who we are. This is a big issue when it comes to the day to day struggle of being TG in a "normal" world.

Unfortunately for us Hollywood and the internet have spent years mis-representing and exploiting pretty much *everyone* who might fall under the umbrella of the "T" in GLBT.

Let's start with Hollywood. By Hollywood I mean predominantly television and movies. For years Hollywood has portrayed (mostly wrongfully) TG people as either freaks or comic relief. Everything from sitcoms and movies about what a joke it is for a man to dress up as a woman for some ulterior motive, such as "getting the girl", to media exploitation of serial killers or other criminals being dressed as women, or "transgender".

I personally have seen multiple news stories where it was claimed by the media that a "man dressed as a woman" perpetrated some kind of crime and the anchors made references to such

Hollywood hits as "Silence of The Lambs". Later, after some digging, I would find out that the man in question was mentally disturbed and wearing something like a bra and panties. This does not constitute being "dressed like a woman" and it definitely does not have anything to do with the TG community.

Some of you may remember the whole "Andrew Cunanan" fiasco. He was a spree killer who killed five people including designer Gianni Versace. This was a media frenzy on our local news (I cannot speak for the rest of the country). Apparently he was a gay man and somewhere, somehow it was put to the media that he might be "dressed as a woman" when the police were hunting him. From that moment on he was referred to almost exclusively as a crossdresser or transsexual killer.

Even if he had been dressed as woman it should not have made any difference or had any bearing on the terrible acts he committed. Men and women kill people all the time and it usually has little to do with their gender. The media however loves to sensationalize. To them it is far more interesting if they make it sound like how the killer was dressed determined that he/she was in fact transgender and that the killer's gender confusion attributed to his/her mental sate and ultimately the killings.

That is pretty much as ridiculous as saying that wearing a red T-shirt obviously meant that a man was psychotic and that is why he went on a killing spree. Wearing women's clothing does not automatically mean a man is transgender nor does actually being transgender automatically make someone mentally deficient. It is wrong of the media to imply these connections simply for the purpose of boosting their ratings.

Another aspect of the Hollywood sensationalization of TG life is the comic relief one. For years they have been churning out movies that blatantly ridicule TG people all in the name of a good laugh for the "straight" folks and to earn a buck. I could cite specific films here but I am not going to. Hollywood gets enough publicity at our expense without adding to it.

I have seen countless movies where it was supposed to be a big joke on the straight guy that the girl he was with turned out to be a transsexual or a guy dressed as a woman. Then the "hero" makes a big vulgar display of how disgusted he is. In some films vomiting, crying and scrubbing himself all over.

Then, of course, there is the aforementioned, "guys dressing as girls" to get close to a woman, get into schools, rent apartments, etc. All getting a good laugh while sending the message to the uninformed public that transsexuals or crossdressers (which many believe are one and the same) are something to laugh.

Then, there are the endless television programs

where "straight" men make jokes about how "gross" it is to accidentally pick up a "chick with a dick". Or, the programs about gay men in drag which send the mixed message that they themselves are transsexuals while at the same time making derogatory statements and jokes about "trannies".

Movies and television are not alone in this sensationalism and bashing either. There is also of course the music industry. I have heard songs negatively referring to transsexuals but the most offensive, and probably the most famous is a song (and its' associated music video) by Aerosmith - "Dude Looks Like A Lady".

Firstly – like Steven Tyler has room to talk about how anyone else looks! "Dude" Looks Like A Zombie.

Secondly, the song is supposed to be about how he picked up a woman in a bar and she turned out to be a "dude" even though she had a gorgeous body, he was so surprised, disgusted, blah, blah same old cliches.

The problem I have with this song is that it became such a huge hit, is still played to death everywhere today, and everyone seems to think that it's funny and OK to play it. Yet, the song by Dire Straights with the line about the "little fagot with the earring and the make-up" is censored now when they play it on the radio.

I personally am not a fan of censorship but if there *is* going to be censorship it should apply to everyone. All minorities should be protected under the law. There should not be instances where it is wrong to offend one group but OK to offend others. Equal rights should mean equal rights for everyone. A good example of this is another hugely famous song by Guns n' Roses which referred to African Americans and homosexuals using derogatory terms which I will not repeat here.. There has been much raving about this song for years and it was pulled from the radio because of the derogatory statement about African Americans, but little to nothing said about the derogatory statement directed at homosexuals.

I saw an interview with W. Axl Rose in which he stated that he "knew that line was going to haunt me for the rest of my life...". So if he *knew* why did he still go through the extensive process of rehearsing, recording, engineering, mastering and ultimately releasing the song with the line in it? Sensationalism. Making a buck. I wonder what his true feelings are on transgendered people?

Then there is "reality" TV. Shows like Jerry Springer and Steve Wilkos. Episode after episode of "trannies". An offensive term in and of itself to many in the TG community. The actual episodes are usually even more offensive, but more importantly, they broadcast a misleading perception of transgenderism to a demographic of viewers who are already ignorant enough to even watch the show in the first place!

I have personally overheard way too many conversations where women boasted about what they would do if some "tranny" stole their man. I have also heard many remarks in these same conversations about how "trannies" are ma stealers and freaks and not to be trusted. Because they saw it on Jerry Springer so it *must* be true.

Also the viewers are not seeing a fair representation of the TG community. If, by some miracle, these shows *are* in fact real (which I do not believe). Then the TG people who choose to appear on these shows are not exactly the "cream of the crop" so to speak.

Certainly there are freaks and nutcases in *any* group, seeking attention and willing to belittle themselves on national television for some money and fifteen minutes of fame, but this does not represent the entire group.

Do you think a wife-beating, child-molesting, skinny little white boy who smokes crack and dropped out of school in the third grade is a fair representation of *all* white American males? Of course not, but they are the *only* ones being portrayed on these shows.

What about the internet and the current trend of "reality" videos? YouTube is simply rampant with cell phone videos of "tranny fights". While I am writing this I just went to YouTube and typed "tranny fight" into the search bar. It says "About 27,500 results". The first page that came up has video titles like "When trannies Go Crazy – Fight Compilation", "Tranny Crackheads Fight It Out", "Straight Men vs Trannies Brawl in FL", and on, and on.

The general public and especially the internet addicted youth of today are over exposed to this unregulated sensationalism and end up perceiving all TG people as these stereotypes when it has been my experience that this is in no way an accurate representation. Many of the videos are taken out of context. They are instances where TG people are attacked and try to defend themselves but the video is shot and edited to look like the situation was different. Then it is titled by someone just trying to get hits on their video page. How do they *know* that these people are on crack? Apparently they followed them from the crack house after personally observing them smoking it. So where is the video of that? What's more, why does this not fall under slander and libelous? Isn't it against the law to accuse someone of a crime without evidence? Last I checked, smoking crack is a crime.

Other videos are not of transsexuals at all. They are simply male prostitutes wearing women's clothing and/or people out looking for trouble. I'm sure many of the videos are completely staged and still more are simply just genetic females getting into trouble. Many of the videos never show any conclusive proof that the participants are anything other than genetic women getting into fights over drugs, men, etc.

The point is that the mainstream media and especially the internet are doing far more harm than good when it comes to the plight of the TG community. We are portrayed on TV and in the movies as unstable freaks and weirdos. Why are there never any movies or television shows made where a random key character just happens to be transgender and acts like a normal everyday person? There are gays in almost every television series on the air today, portrayed for the most part as normal, accepted people, but how many transgender people?

This brings me to another issue that was discussed on the internet recently: a serious lack of transgender people playing themselves in the movies.

It was mentioned that it seems *every* time a movie is made where a transgender person is featured, that Hollywood goes out of the way to either cast a very masculine man in a female-to-male role or a gorgeous genetic female starlet. There is no shortage of extremely talented real-life transgender people out there who would love to play the parts and represent the community.

I have noticed that Hollywood seems to like to cast female-to-male TG roles in serious dramas with masculine straight men in dresses (apparently because they feel the audience should see their expectation on the screen) and beautiful genetic female starlets as transwomen in the comedies. Again, sensationalism.

Then there is the porn industry, specifically the online porn industry. It is no secret that I have been a shemale porn star fro many years, but I have tried to maintain some sense of class and decency and produce and release my own videos. I refer to myself as shemale in the videos and titles because, as I said before, this is how I identify with my gender.

I have never done a video for another producer or company and do not condone other producer's use of terms like "tranny". I originally got into making adult videos for a source of income and because it was fun. Sex is fun, that's why it is so popular. That is why the Earth is currently faced with a serious over population problem. Everybody does it. Some of us just record it and sell it from time to time.

There seems to be a serious misconception among the general population about porn. People seem to think that because a video was viewed a million times or sold a million copies that the performers in the video had sex that many times. I just don't know what to say about that. Apparently they also think that every time a Seinfeld episode is re-run the actors actually act out the show again.

Of all the videos I have made and released, in them I have only had sex with four different people. I know people who have been *married* more times than that! Also, all of the people that co-starred with me in the videos were close personal friends or significant others that I was in a long term relationship with.

The idea that porn stars are loose, nympho-maniacal, sluts running around screwing everything that moves, both on and off screen is a total misconception. In my case at least. As I have repeatedly stated, I speak for myself from my experience and point of view. I can not speak for everyone in the mainstream adult industry but I somehow think the majority of them are not too different from me.

Porn is after all, all about fantasy. It is not reality. It is not a fair representation of love, or of relationships. It is all about fun with sex.

Here is where the problem comes in. Just like with the sensationalized "reality" videos on YouTube, impressionable people view porn on the internet and have a tendency to perceive it as an accurate portrayal of real life.

Also, unfortunately, it seems that most people curious about the TG world use porn as basis of comparison. This I believe is a major influence on the general public's perception of transgender people, culminating in an accepted belief that all TG people are "trannies" and that all of these "trannies" are prostitutes, sluts, etc.

There is a dilemma here. When I got into making and selling adult videos I was on the verge of homelessness because I had been led to believe that it was OK to "come out" and be myself. This instead resulted in blatant discrimination and loss of regular employment. I couldn't get a job to save my life. I ended up with the same two choices that many, many transwomen over the years have ended up with – prostitution or porn. I chose porn. I have never been and will *never* be a prostitute.

Over the years my royalties from adult videos sustained me pretty well and kept me from ending up on the street. That is until the recent financial crisis which is a completely separate issue.

All of this brings me back to one of my earlier points about the separation of gender identity and sex or other aspects of day to day life.

There are far more genetic female adult video performers than there are transgender ones. This is what I mean about everybody being equal. Straight women and men do porn. Straight women and men become lawyers, police officers, bank robbers, etc. So all this complaining on the internet about our "image" is completely ridiculous. Does one "straight" man becoming a porn star or robbing a bank ruin the image of the entire "straight community"? Of course not. So one TG posting racey pictures on Facebook should not affect the entire TG community negatively. If all people should be regarded as equal then all people should be allowed the same achievements and faults equally. If a man is hero or a criminal then he should be treated as a hero or a criminal, if a transgendered person is a hero or a criminal then they should be treated as a hero or a criminal, no a *transgendered* hero or criminal.

I find it truly sad though that transgender people (particularly male-to-female) and people like myself are basically forced to turn to either porn or prostitution to survive. Something definitely needs to be done about this very soon. There needs to be not only legislation protecting us from discrimination but some kind of active support to help us find jobs and careers. I have searched endlessly online for transgender support groups and have found pretty much nothing but emotional support. That is fine and I'm sure well needed by some, but many of us need real support. Hands on help with employment, insurance, finances, etc.

It can be increasingly difficult to find employers who are actively hiring TG people, especially online. It seems like every time you type in a search with the term transgender in it you get nothing but emotional support groups, pages about hormones and GRS experiences or porn.

Another hurdle we face is discrimination even if legislation is passed. There are always ways around everything and employers are experts at finding loopholes. I have been repeatedly denied employment because of my gender identity but you will never find a written record to corroborate this. An employer would have to be a complete idiot to give me in writing the real reason for a denial of employment.

All any employer has to say is that there are no available positions, there was a better candidate with more experience, you are "over qualified" (my favorite), etc. Florida is a "Right To Work State" which basically means employers have the right to deny employment to you without reason and fire you for no reason at all.

I have even tried to get jobs by dressing and acting like a regular male and been denied because the prospective employer would look at me with that all too familiar look that says they know what I am and don't like it.

This brings me back tot he discrimination within the GLBT community. I have never been able to get a job in any gay establishments either. Not even in the bars or clubs that I frequent where they know me. I have seen unreliable gay men and lesbians come and go while repeatedly asking about the positions. They always seem to hire the "cute" gay guys and I cannot recall *ever* having seen another TG or intersexed person like myself in any of those positions. The closest thing would be the drag queens performing in the shows. Which brings me to the next point.

I have never been able to perform in the drag

shows either. I am an established internet personality with a huge world wide following, a published and accomplished musician and performer with extensive stage experience and internationally released chart topping album, an internet radio show hostess, a porn star (and somewhat of an icon in the fetish community) and a published author. Yet I can't even get into an amateur talent competition on a weeknight with amateurs who can barely lip sync other people's songs! Why? Because I am not actually a *drag queen* apparently.

I have no great desire to perform in drag shows and even less to lip sync. I prefer to perform actual live music of my own. I just want to express the point that discrimination is rampant inside the GLBT community especially toward the TG community.

This brings me to the next subject. Discrimination in the world of "straight' or "normal" music.

SIX

As I mentioned earlier in the book, I have seen my share of discrimination toward TG people in the music industry.

Not long ago I conducted a little social experiment mostly within the local music scene where I live. In this experiment I used two separate but equal profiles: one was a straight male rock/metal performer, the other myself.

I created online profiles for both, with pictures, videos, music samples,etc. The music samples were different but equal in quality and composition. This was easy to accomplish because I wrote and recorded the music for both using all the same equipment and settings.

I then set about answering advertisements placed all over the internet for bands that were seeking a lead guitarist with my particular, style, influences, equipment,etc. Many of these ads claimed to be open to males or females. I answered literally hundreds of ads in my area, thousands nationwide.

I first answered these ads as myself, explaining who I was in great detail and giving directions to my online music and video samples, and pictures. I directed people to my Reverbnation profile   I (currently have over 24,000 song plays and over 5,000 fans and steadily climbing) where I have been lingering around the very top of the metal charts for all of Hollywood, CA. I also sent them to my profile on the Indie Music charts (which is like the Billboard charts for unsigned musicians) where, at the time I was in the top twenty metal artists in the entire world.

I also had dozens of other online music profiles with thousands of fans and followers and was receiving airplay on countless internet radio stations.

To this day I have not received one single reply. Not even a rejection.

I then answered all the same ads using the male profile which had fewer fans, fewer plays and less exposure all around. I received replies from all but a few, quickly and most wanting me to join their bands sight unseen right away. You can draw your own conclusions from this information but I have already drawn mine!

Needless to say I did not join any of these bands. For one thing I certainly do not want to have to disguise myself as a man just to play in someone else's band (I spent enough years doing that in bands that I formed myself!) and for another I don't want to associate with people who are bigoted against TG people.

For the non-musician readers out there let me explain a little about artists like myself. I personally, as a musician, have no desire to play music if I am not enjoying what I am doing. If I wanted to do something mundane, disappointing, stressful, aggravating and monotonous simply for money I would just get a regular day job.

Also, music, real, good, music that comes from the heart has feeling to it. If you are not enjoying it or not enjoying playing with the other members of a band then the music is going to suck. It is going to sound mechanical at best.

I was exposed to music at a very young age and instantly fell in love with every aspect of it. I began receiving musical instruction at a very young age which continued all through school from kindergarten into college.

When I got my first guitar and started teaching myself how to play it I was forced to take my knowledge of music theory from school and figure out how to apply it to the guitar myself. I have never taken a single guitar lesson.

Aerosmith was one of my biggest early influences and made me want to become a rock star. You may be able to imagine my disappointment when they released "Dude Looks Like A Lady". I didn't listen to them much after that. One of the great disappointments of growing up is finding out what kind of people your heroes really are. If I am a hero to anyone I certainly hope reading this book does not disappoint them or change the way they see me in a negative way. I have never intentionally misled anyone who may have looked up to me or looked to me for inspiration.

Anyway, returning to the topic of discrimination toward the TG community in the music industry, I was also officially solicited by a major record company (who shall also remain nameless) under the male persona and profile. Not once, but *twice* in about a three month period. Bands and musicians can play, record, tour, promote and struggle their entire lifetimes without ever getting solicited (which means officially asked to submit a music demo and press kit to see if the label wants to move forward with contract negotiations – signing you to their label) which for most is basically the Holy Grail of the music industry.

Now it should be understood that in the grand scheme of things, especially in today's music industry, getting solicited and getting your demo in tot he big wigs doesn't mean *that* much. While it is a pretty big deal it still is no guarantee that you are going to get a record deal and become a huge overnight success.

The way it works (or is supposed to) these days, is once they listen to your demo and have their eye on you, you still have to spend some time (usually a couple of years) proving to them that you could be a big cash generator. You accomplish this by touring and promoting as best you can, on your own dime unless you happen to have connections with money, and build your following and popularity. Then, once *you* have done all the hard work and built up enough of a reputation and following that people are guaranteed to spend money to see you play live and by your merchandise, the record label may make you an offer. Basically, once you have already made it on your own and they see that they can make money on you without really doing much, then they want to step in and take over.

Since (as a man anyway) I really had no financing and no way to accomplish this on my own I had no real expectations of hearing from them after I sent in my demo and press kit. Big surprise, I never did.

Now, as myself, with far more exposure, a much larger fan base, more airplay, and literally thousands of followers worldwide already in place from my distinguished career in modeling, adult videos, etc., I was never *once* contacted or solicited.

As myself I have an album released worldwide, a very large and continually growing fan base, extremely marketable music and image, especially in the big money making gay club scene, and have been receiving hundreds of rave reviews. I basically have the whole package that the major labels are always on the look out for.

So why do all my emails go unanswered? Why I

have I not been solicited by a major record label? Why I have I not been invited to participate in big tours and festivals? I have seen literally hundreds of musicians with fewer followers, less exposure and lower quality music receive all of these things through all of the same networking.

So why not me? Probably just the luck of the draw right? Then why *did* I receive all those same offers as the *same* person with the *same* quality music and *less* exposure and promoting through the *same* networks presenting my image as a *male?*

I'm sure there is some reasonable explanation behind it and any other conclusion would just be paranoia on my part. Right?

I don't want the reader to think that I am bitter or whining. I am just stating the facts to try to express the resistance that I personally have met as me in the music industry and the world in general.

In a way though it is probably a good thing that I was never picked up as a recording artist. After seeing the truth about the financial side of the big music industry I'm not so sure I would want to be apart of it now anyway. It seems that no one is really making any money except the big labels. The artists seem to be treated like owned dog an pony acts that are thrown just enough scraps and fame to keep them happy then ultimately cast aside when their sales drop a little.

On top of that you have all the drugs, drama,

scandal and lack of privacy issues. The endless schmoozing and selling out. It seems like yo make a deal with the Devil, sell your soul and have to become a complete phony or you get black listed and cast out.

The entertainment industry is so hypocritical besides. What is a major selling point one day is unacceptable behavior the next. I'm sure they would exploit the fact that I am a shemale porn star to get sales up then a little while later get rid of me because, oh my God, I'm a *shemale* and a *porn star!*

Plus, I don't want to end up on Dancing With The Stars.

During the years that I was "undercover" playing out locally in bands as a male I learned a lot about how many (local anyway) musicians feel.

It is amazing to me just how superficial people can be, even "open minded" musicians who spend most of their time seemingly trying to convince whoever will listen just how deep and open minded they are.

I have seen it on television with the big Hollywood performers, always bragging about how they fight for diversity, they are so open minded, hey are fighting to stop discrimination, hunger, alien abductions, whatever.

It has been my experience that local musicians say pretty much the same things. It is difficult to say if this is because they are the same kind of people as the big stars or if they are just emulating the big stars' behavior because they believe the same behavior is expected of them by society. Either way, they behave pretty much the same and make the same claims.

Now, what they *claim* and what they actually *believe* or *feel* often turn out to be completely different things!

As I have stated, I am speaking from personal experience and actual personal interaction with these people. I am not relating third party information or hearsay.

It has been my experience that people in general (again in the area where I grew up at least) tend to automatically jump to the conclusion that because you *look* like them, *dress* like them and hang around with them, that you share the same thoughts and feeling as them. This in turn lulls them into a false sense of security, or maybe its camaraderie, which in turn causes them to express their true inner feelings. They seem to feel that you are one of the gang or club and they can say how they really feel around you because they believe *you* share their beliefs.

This is what I mean when I say that going out dressed as a man and interacting with these people is basically like undercover work. I worked for years as a fully licensed investigator and I have extensive undercover experience. I have found that (for me anyway) the best way to get information is to dress the part and say as little as possible. Since most people seem to suffer from "pressure of speech" all you have to do is keep your mouth shut long enough and they will tell you their whole life story just to hear *someone* talking.

Probably partly out of force of habit, this carried over into my everyday life and by just letting everyone else do the talking I have learned things that therapists, doctors, priests and spouses will never hear from people.

I can actually go to a social gathering, club, bar, what have you, dress to blend in and just walk up to any random little group engaged in conversation with a drink in my hand and an air of belonging and listen to everything they have to say without them even getting suspicious.

This is basically what has happened to me for years whenever I went anywhere dressed as a man and this is how I found out the true feelings of many people on the issues of transgenderism, gays, lesbians, the TG world and many other topics.

Bar rooms are great for this especially since alcohol tends to act like a truth serum! Sometimes I would even plant the seed to get a topic to come up that I was curious about people's views on. This is incredibly easy, especially If there has recently been some media hype about the topic that pretty much everyone has heard. All you have to do is blurt out one quick little remark like, "Hey! Did you see that story on the news about the transsexual getting beat up? Wild."

Next thing you know the train is off and running and they can't shut up about it for the next thirty minutes or so. As I mentioned earlier, I do not drink or take drugs of any kind, so I have my complete faculties while the buzzed to inebriated talkers ramble on. I always like to have a soda or something in my hand too because then they (once again!) just assume I'm drinking and I am as drunk as they are.

Hey, we're all drinking buddies here, we can speak freely!

I never even have to conceal the fact that I don't drink to quell their paranoia. It seems no matter how many times I tell people I don't drink, they don't seem to hear it and keep offering to buy me drinks.

Anyway, now that I have explained *how* I have heard many of the things I have heard, let me talk about *what* I have heard.

It has been my experience that these self-proclaimed, open minded individuals in the music scene (since this is local I will refer to it as the scene instead of the industry) aren't always as open minded as they would like the general public to believe.

As far as the local music scene is concerned I have heard so many people proclaim their acceptance of diversity and TG people, etc. I have seen them post all kinds of things online on their social networks about how they believe in equality and everyone needs to love everybody, blah, blah.

I have seen these same musicians perform at and promote diversity benefits, specifically inclusive of the TG community.

I have personally listened to these same musicians make sadistic jokes in low voices about gays, lesbians, TG people, etc and bash the hell out of them behind their backs.

One specific incident that is burned into my mind and always will be, I was a front row witness to. I went to support a (now former) "friend's" band at a gig then went to breakfast with them at one of those all night places, a Denny's I believe.

While we were sitting there, one of the band members happened to notice a small group of crossdressers sitting at another table.

Laughing the entire time, he made crude jokes about them, and even taunted them, trying to provoke a reaction out of them. The rest of the band laughed along with him and a few of them even joined in. I tried to get them to stop, without being too obvious and failed, so I then changed subject and drew their attention to another subject that caused them to lose interest in the crossdressers who got up and left.

I was, of course, furious but in the spirit of de-escalating the situation, I smiled and politely kept my mouth shut.

When we were leaving, out in the parking lot the

band member who had instigated the whole scene made a remark about how he should have kicked their asses. I told him that would have been a bad move since I had worked with one of them and he was an ex-Marine and currently a police officer. The band member's face went white and he said, "Oh shit!"

I lied of course. I had actually seen them around at the clubs but had no idea who any of them really were. I did however plant that seed in his mind that he should watch his mouth because you just never know *who* someone really is.

The best part of this little story? The bigoted, hateful band memeber, who is still the same person and still playing the scene today, plays all of the diversity benefits and I have even heard him make speeches on the mic about acceptance and everyone doing their part, then get off the stage and talk about "fagots".

None of them were ever really my friends and after that night I never spoke to any of them again. I did unfortunately run into them in the bars/clubs from time to time.

I also got to listen first hand to many of the bands/musicians whose online ads I had answered as myself (they not knowing I was the same person) and been passed over, talk negatively about TG people. No big surprise there.

I don't want the reader to think that I am bitter and just totally bashing all musicians. I have met my fare share of local musicians who truly are accepting of TG people and are not two faced. It has been unfortunate for me though that their musical tastes run in different directions than mine so, due to creative differences, I never got involved with any of them musically.

Sadly though too, these people are far outnumbered by the local musicians who *do* have issues with TG people. I really didn't want this book to be all negative or sound like I am complaining and bitter. Right now I am just relating some of the negative experiences I have had to cope with growing up as me in the area where I have lived for so long.

I am not a morose, dark, morbid, gloomy person! I love being me and (aside from the problems brought about recently by the financial crisis) I am generally a very happy, fun, energetic, optimistic, playful person. I have some pretty great friends, I go out and have fun whenever I can afford to do so and I interact with a lot of interesting and nice people. Maybe I should talk some about that to lighten the mood!

SEVEN

As I mentioned before, I usually go out to GLBT clubs when I go out. I have known a lot of transsexuals who don't go to these clubs. I have also heard many transsexuals bash the gay community just like I have heard many members of the gay community bash transsexuals and other members of the TG community.

I am very personable and outgoing and get a long with a lot of people from all genders and all walks of life. I also do not stop being friends with my friends because one individual or members of one group don't like them.

Many of my close friends are gay men. They are nice, fun, people who genuinely accept me for who I am and *none* of them bash anyone in the TG community.

Some of my friends are also drag queens who do not bash members of the TG community either. Just because a select few talk negatively on TV and the internet about TG people for their own personal gain does not mean they *all* do.

Some of my friends are crossdressers, some are transsexuals, some never define themselves to me and I don't ask how they perceive themselves. I accept them for who they are and I am not the least bit nosy about it.

So many people sun around claiming to be truly accepting and non-prejudicial, then proceed to ask all kinds of invasive questions about who or (ugh!) "what" (I cringe) someone is.

I truly do not have that urge. When I meet people I meet the *person* and I am not the least bit curious about how they perceive themselves, or who they feel they are at heart.

This is not to say that I am uninterested in them and their lives or that I am dismissive and don't care. I am interested in the *person*.

I can't even count how many times I've met someone truly engaging, had great conversations with them all night and never even thought to ask them their name!

Anyway, if someone wants to tell me about themselves then they will tell me. It is really none of my business if they view themselves as transgender, transsexual, gay, straight, bi-sexual, lesbian, and so on. I don't need to satisfy some deep-seated curiosity about whether they are taking hormones or undergoing surgery. If they feel like mentioning it they will.

As I mentioned earlier in the book, I go to the gay clubs because they are fun, more laid back and more enjoyable than the testosterone fueled bars full of insecure "straight" men who feel the need to be rude, crude and prove their manhood. I can't stand that. It's still amazes me how many women actually find that kind of behavior attractive around here. I've always believed that grown men should behave like gentlemen and not start fights and have belching contests in public places. Especially places full of ladies. Maybe I'm being old fashioned, but I think everyone should behave with some level of class and dignity when out in public. Being yourself and doing your own thing doesn't mean you have to be completely un-civilized.

As I was saying, I like to go out and have fun. When I do I like to go where I can relax and have fun and not have to worry about unnecessary drama or incurring hatred from the ignorant. In a perfect world that would be everywhere, but, alas, we do not live in a perfect world.

Like I said, I often meet a lot of nice, and interesting people when I go out. I often spend hours engaged in interesting conversations with people about everyday things, just like any other "normal" person. I don't spend my time continually thinking to myself about my gender identity. I just do my thing and be myself just like any person born into any specific gender and who I am is who I am. That's one of the upsides to hanging out in places full of accepting people. Gender issues don't come up unless someone else brings them up.

Part of what is making writing this so difficult is that I *don't* walk around everyday consciously aware of my gender and asking myself questions like, *am I male? Am I female? Am I transsexual? Am I a transvestite? Am I a crossdresser?* Etc. I don't have those issues or inner conflicts or doubts. I know exactly who I am and it is not and issue with *me*. If it is an issue with *others* then I suggest they get themselves some therapy to learn how to deal with it. Because of this I have to really dig down and think hard about what to say and how to say it and what topics to cover.

I mentioned early on a difference between gender identity and sexual orientation. I don't know what the psychologists would say but I believe one has very little to do with the other. I know in my case neither has anything to do with the other. As I said before, I felt my gender identity long before I ever had any sexual feelings at all.

To say that because someone is a male to female transsexual, she should be attracted to men, totally negates being born homosexual. By that reasoning all men should be attracted to women and all women should be attracted to men. This would dictate that homosexuality is a *choice* of some kind.

So, if men can be born attracted to other men and women can be born attracted to other women then female to male transsexuals can be born attracted to men and male to female transsexuals can be born attracted to women. Right?

What about bi-sexuality? If men and women can be born attracted to both sexes then so can transsexuals. If men and women can be born attracted to transsexuals then transsexuals can be born attracted to transsexuals.

If your school of thought is that sexual orientation is a *preference* what changes?

Instead of saying men and women can be *born* attracted to their own genders or all three genders and you say that men and women can simply *prefer* all three genders the end result is the same: transsexuals can too.

I don't know what the predominant school of thought on sexual orientation is at the moment, as I have declared from the beginning I am not a therapist or doctor or expert of any kind, but either way whatever is acceptable for males and females also should be acceptable for transsexuals.

Speaking for myself I am attracted sexually to men women and TGs, although not as much to genetic women.

Now I am not talking about love or relationships or anything, I am talking strictly physical, sexual attraction. To me there is more to a person than their outward physical appearance and who they are as a *person* is the predominant determining factor in whether I find them"sexy" or not.

I am not into casual, anonymous, sexual encounters. I like to get to know someone first and that goes a long way to determining if I am ever going to have sex with them.

Safe sex is not just putting on a condom. Safe sex is knowing who you're doing it with.

It is easy to see how confusing the whole TG world can be when you start peeling away the layers and delving into the various aspects of it. I personally am not big on all the labels and sub-categories. I am not even sure who came up with most of them and who is out there deciding who is who.

When the average lay-person (outside the TG community) is confronted with all of these sub-categories and different aspects it must be even more difficult for them to comprehend. This I imagine is what generates all questions that many TG people construe as rude.

How can we expect outsiders to our community to automatically understand the differences between crossdressers, drag queens, transvestites, drag kings, transsexuals, shemales, transgendered and intersexed when they are not readily educated about the differences and many of us don't even know the differences?

It seems to me like almost every TG I meet has a completely different definition of themselves when compared to the "standard" definitions. I meet people calling themselves "queens" who fit the "traditional" definition of crossdresser more and people who identify as crossdressers who fit the "traditional" definition of transvestites more.

Like I said, I don't care for the whole labeling thing but if it *is* going to be used don't you think someone should possibly help these people within our community learn and understand these definitions so that they can learn more about themselves and figure out who they are? Rather than belittle and berate them for describing themselves with what you perceive as the *wrong* label? Leave the hateful comments tot he haters. We have enough to deal with as it is!

There has been a heated argument on the internet of late about just exactly *who* falls under the umbrella of the TG community or the "T" in GLBT.

As far as I am concerned anyone who expresses themselves as the opposite gender to which they were labeled at birth does. This means anyone who regularly lives and presents themselves as the opposite sex and anyone born intersexed. If a crossdresser feels comfortable presenting his or her self as the opposite gender on a regular basis they are included. Transsexuals are included. Intersexed people are included. People who feel they are trapped in the body of the opposite sex yet do not dress in the clothes of the opposite sex (or if they do) are included. Drag queens that dress full time or are not just doing drag as a job are included, along with many others who are spread through out the gray areas.

I am not saying that these people should all fit some legal definition of the "T" or of "TG" or that they should be accepted by anyone else. I am saying that *I* personally accept these people as member of the TG community and if *you* do not then that's your problem. No one is going to tell me who I can accept and who I can't. No one is going to tell me who is who. I am not going to discriminate based on other's opinions.

Getting back to sexual orientation (or preference if you prefer!), as I have stated, I see at as having no bearing on gender. In my case at least I know this to be true.

It seems strange to me that sexual orientation is such a big deal today in this country. It doesn't bother me at all to see a man and woman holding hands, kissing, etc. So why does it bother so many of them to see two men together, two women together, a man with a transsexual? Apparently some of them believe that children seeing this will be confused and wrongfully drawn to the opposite gender?

I don't believe that at all. My sexual orientation was not influenced in that way at all. In fact I didn't even know what gay or lesbian meant until long after I started having sexual urges. From the time I started thinking about sex I was attracted to both males and females. I had never even seen a gay porno or a gay couple, etc. I had absolutely no exposure to anything like that . I just knew that I was attracted to both sexes.

Perhaps some people who are born homosexual get confused by societal pressure to be "straight" and spend a lifetime trying to figure out if they are gay, straight or bisexual. I don't really know. All I do know is that I did not have that conflict. I have known from a very young age who I was attracted to and although I may have kept it hidden from everyone else, I never hid it from myself.

I have had steady relationships with men, women and TGs and the only thing missing sexually in any of those relationships was the penis. I have found over years of experimenting that although I am sexually attracted to both the male and female form I prefer someone with a penis as opposed to a vagina.

If this makes me gay in the eyes of those analytical people out there then so be it. I am a gay shemale. I am also more attracted to other people like me (shemales) than I am to regular men. So if I am the third sex (as I refer to it) and I am attracted to my same sex then I guess that also maxes me a homosexual shemale.

Judge me all you want. I will not defend who I am, nor will I make any apologies for not meeting *your* expectation of who you think I should be or how you think I should identify myself.

So there you have it. My sexual orientation set apart from my gender identity. My sexual orientation does not define my gender anymore than the color of my eyes or my favorite food does. Does just naturally being a dog or cat person determine whether you have breasts or a penis, or vice versa? Isn't that kind of like saying, "You eat three meals a day, you must be a guy." ?

So I think it is safe to say that a lack of education on the subject and media hype/sensationalization contribute greatly to the general public's confusion on the whole issue of who is actually considered TG and who TG people really are.

What is probably needed most is to educate the general public on the difference between reality and fantasy. As I have heard, time and time again, many members of the general population use internet porn and the exploitative media as their guide to understanding the TG community.

They are being bombarded with fantasy and misinformation and interpreting it as real. It is not a real and fair representation of the TG community, but, to those who do not understand this, it presents all TG people as sluts, whores, perverts, and fetishists. They do not stop to think that "straight" porn presents genetic females and males in all the same roles. People are people and how they behave sexually or as a person in general has nothing to do with their gender identity. A male, female or TG person can all be nice, cruel, gay, straight, perverse, ignorant, educated, loving, dismissive, prejudiced, accepting, kinky, weird, funny, boring, etc.

If the general public was educated to this fact somehow I believe it would be a big help!

For us to be accepted as individuals and as *people* by the general public people first need to learn the difference between what a person *does* and who a person is. They need to understand that just because one member of a specific gender, race or social group behaves in what they perceive as an unacceptable fashion that not every member of that group is predisposed to behave in that same fashion.

Recent examples of this media fueled, knee jerk negative response are the molestation charges against Catholic priests and school teachers. A few years ago when several priests were accused of molesting altar boys I personally witnessed such a reaction. It seemed like everywhere I went people were spouting off about what perverts *all* Catholic priests were. The media fueled this fire by going on witch hunts to publicize as many cases as possible and find other "despicable" acts by priests and church cover ups. I saw news coverage where the reporters tried to make things like traffic violations or unpaid parking tickets by clergy sound like murders. I saw news coverage where reporters talked about doing background investigations on priests and blurted out phrases like, "Do *you* know who's preaching in *your* neighborhood church?"

Once again, all in the name of sensationalism.

They purposely made it sound like *all* Catholic priests were perverts and sex offenders and not to be trusted. Ultimately, innocent priests around the nation suffered because of the alleged actions of a few. I know from personal experience that absolutely *none* of the priests in any of the churches I attended growing up every committed any such acts and never would.

The same thing happens with teachers every time one teacher molests a student or is even just accused of molesting a student, suddenly there is a national call to arms to investigate every educator in the country. The practical truth is that anyone applying for any kind of position like teaching should undergo an extensive background investigation prior to employment. I personally have had to have statewide and federal criminal background checks, credit checks, psychological exams, personality tests, drug testing, past employer interviews and friend and neighbor interviews about my *character* just get part time jobs lifting the gate and saying hello to rich people coming and going from their little gated communities! I had no interaction with minors and no access of any kind to anything of any value. I couldn't even have entered or burglarized any of the homes if I wanted because they all had separate high tech security systems linked directly to local law enforcement!

Which brings me to another great example – law

enforcement. The Rodney King incident springs to mind. Every time a few select police officers go too far, or just outright break the law, suddenly everyone hates *all* cops.

I have worked with a lot of police officers and the majority of them have all been very honorable, open minded, fair people. Some of them have even been gay or lesbian and a personal friend of mine was a transsexual. To hate all law enforcement officers because a very select few, wearing the same uniform, behaved badly is ridiculous. How much are you going to hate them when someone is trying to kill you and you have to call 9-1-1?

There have also been quite a number of these cases where men *impersonating* police officers were pulling over cars and raping women. The media used this opportunity (again local to my area at least) to tell women not to pull over when they saw flashing lights behind them and to call 9-1-1 and or drive to a well lit public area before pulling over. This resulted in quite a mess as you can imagine. Women were getting arrested and I believe in some cases shot and killed, for evading police and resisting arrest. An intended warning for a missing tail light ends up as a police chase and shooting death.

This is a great example to try to further my point. In the TG community (as I and many others see it anyway) there are many different subgroups as I have mentioned before; crossdressers, transsexuals, drag queens, transvestites, etc. Within these subgroups, in fact within the entire TG community, as with *any* community, there will undoubtedly be bad apples.

Just like how someone falling under the umbrella of law enforcement, or someone *posing* as law enforcement, wearing the same uniform as it were, can turnout to be a criminal, so can the same situation arise within other groups. If a criminal dresses up like a police officer and rapes women society should understand that the all the police in the country had nothing to do with it. If a man dresses up as a woman and commits a crime or behaves in a manner unbecoming, all TG people should not be viewed the same way. If one crossdesser engages in prostitution, does drugs, or exposes himself in public, *all* crossdressers should not be viewed by the TG community as a bad example and society should not judge the entire TG community based on that one example. If a particular transvestite gets his thrills by going out in public wearing revealing fetish clothing and behaving in a socially unacceptable manner it should not reflect on the *entire* TG community.

Which brings me to my next subject: the fetish world, the fetish community, B&D/S&M, how it is also separate from gender identity and discrimination within these groups.

EIGHT

I personally did not really discover the bondage and fetish world until I was well out of high school and deep into life as myself. I had flipped through the occasional B&D (Bondage and Domination) or fetish magazine and when I got on the internet stumbled across the picture and video sites there. I found some of it quite a turn on. Good, wholesome, kinky fun. Fantasy to spice things up in the bedroom, that sort of thing. I had partners who I engaged in it with and we had a lot of fun.

I did not, however, find out just *how* serious some people in the fetish community do take things until I really got immersed in the whole sub-culture surrounding this world.

For me it is harmless fun to spice things up and have great sexual experiences with other people looking for the same thing. For some people it is much, much deeper than that. For them it can be a complete lifestyle or an obsession. In some cases a very un-healthy obsession.

It is like anything else I imagine, sports, cars, eating, music. Some people just get really involved and obsessed and can take it way too seriously.

Too seriously for my tastes at least.

I personally found this to be true first in the fetish world then later in the B&D world.

When I first got on the internet I set about trying to find other TG people and groups and information. I joined chatrooms and social networks, set up online profiles etc. I took some pictures of myself and posted them to my profiles just like other people did and tried to make local friends in some of the TG chatrooms that I could eventually hang out with in real life. All the standard procedures of the time. Keep in mind this was long ago, before the chatrooms became havens for sexual predators and serial killers. Back when dinosaurs roamed the earth.

Very quickly I began to develop a sort of cult following within the TG community. Everyone loved my pictures, told me how great I looked, etc. Right away I found that there was a huge audience of people, not just in the TG community, but men and women alike who loved my legs and seeing my pictures. This in turn led to the discovery that there was a *huge* (and I do mean HUGE) world wide audience of pantyhose "fetishists" out there that would pay just to see pictures of me wearing pantyhose with short dresses and skirts.

The most common definition I can find today of fetish is: any object or non-genital part of the body that causes habitual erotic response or fixation. I have also heard and read elsewhere that for something to truly be considered a fetish sexual arousal or at least achievement of sexual gratification, or orgasm, must be impossible without the object of the fetish present or involved.

In other words it's not really a fetish if you can have sex and achieve orgasm without it.

I personally (as do many others in the fetish community) broaden my personal definition of a fetish to include not people who simply enjoy regularly to those who cannot live without it. So when I refer to members of the pantyhose fetish community or lifestyle I am including admirers, wearers, etc who just love pantyhose and find them sexually arousing.

This is really a very broad ranging group including men who simply love to see pantyhose on women or TG's, women and men who love to wear them during sex, crossdressers and transvestites who love to wear them all the time, people into pantyhose bondage, and so on.

Now as I have stated before people of all genders are members of this group as well. There are also members of this group who, like the B&D group, or sports fans, take it much too seriously and may go overboard with their obsession. Again, this does not mean anyone with a pantyhose fetish is a sexual deviant or "weird". It's actually quite harmless, healthy fun and spices things up a bit.

Because of my fondness for wearing pantyhose and the positive reaction of so many people to seeing me in them, I was drawn into this whole sub-culture and quickly became something of an icon. Due to a lack of available work and the discrimination I was facing on a daily basis I decided to capitalize on my popularity and have some fun a the same time. I signed on with an amateur adult video company that was just up and coming and started shooting and releasing my own adult videos with a common theme of featuring me in pantyhose. A star was born!

Eventually I started to make fairly decent money from the royalties and didn't have to live on the streets. My following grew day by day and I went from hanging out in the chatrooms to hosting my own chatrooms where I was able to interact with literally thousands of fetishists many of them TG people. I ended up hearing personal accounts/stories from thousands of transsexuals, crossdressers, transvestites, etc about things they wouldn't or couldn't even tell their spouses, doctors or therapists. I found that the numbers of men who crossdress and of people who are transgender are exponentially higher than what all the public surveys claim. The polls and surveys that all the "experts" use to gather their information about how many of us there are aren't even close. I can't give you an exact number but my guess would be to take whatever numbers the "experts" currently have and multiply that by at least two or three.

The big problem with gathering this information

accurately is that so many of us are "closeted" or living in such fear of persecution, ridicule and ostricization that the thought of telling *anyone* about it is too horrifying to even think about.

This brings me back to my earlier example of "being undercover".

Dressed as a man in the "straight" world was basically like being undercover and because they thought I was "one of the boys" people would spill their true feelings and opinions in front of me.

This basically works both ways. As *myself* I'm not undercover, I actually *am* "one of the gurls" but the same principles apply. People are more likely to open up to one of their own.

Now here's what I believe to be the true difference why I have had more deep interactions with members of the TG community than most others: the "closet" factor.

The same fear of exposure and persecution that drives so many TG people underground also keeps them from interacting with each other. This coupled with all the day to day problems of life and in many cases, keeping a low profile, severely limits the number of TG people out there who are initiating contact. Many are rather introverted and very cautious people. I am very outgoing. I readily engage other TG's (and people in general) in conversation and don't hide anything from them. The result is that I am one of the group, available and willing to break the ice and engage others in conversation.

I have been to TG support chatrooms where there were literally hundreds of chatters in the room and *none* of them would talk to each other until I started prompting them.

Another factor that I believe may have contributed to the lack of communication was all the anonymity and phony profiles. I was always very public on the internet with plenty of pictures, videos and personal info on all of my profiles so that people knew I wasn't a fake or an internet "lurker".

Anyway, this is how I learned that a large number of crossdressers, transvestites and transsexuals were (and are) pantyhose and nylon fetishists. I have heard thousands of personal stories about how their fetishes for pantyhose, panties, stockings, women's clothes, etc., led to crossdressing or how being born truly female and dressing the part led to their fetishes. So when "experts" say that experimenting with mommies undies leads to fetishism, leads to crossdressing, leads to transgenderism, that is not really always the case. I have known many genetic females who were born and raised female, dressed female then much later in life developed pantyhose or nylon fetishes. In fact many of the one I have known have said to me that when they were growing up they either hated wearing them or just never really wore them. Then later in life when they were experimenting with them, introducing them into sexual situations, they developed a love for them.

The same holds true for any gender. Any person of any gender identity can develop any fetish. They're gender identity is not necessarily a result of their fetish.

Now for people like myself the fetish world of pantyhose, corsets, lingerie, etc., is just good clean fun and not an obsession. What about those for whom it *is* an obsession? Possibly even to the point where it becomes a problem?

Say there is a straight man who has, for whatever reason, developed a fetish for women's feet. Say then that he becomes so obsessed with women's feet that he follows women around watching their feet and masturbating. Then, for whatever reason, he becomes so obsessed that he begins attacking women, holding them down and rubbing his penis on their feet. Does this now mean that *every* straight man with what is probably the most popular fetish is a dangerous pervert? Of course not and it is pretty much a guarantee that the story would be reported as describing one sick individual with a problem.

Now, let's say a man dressed as a woman were to do the exact same thing. Then the entire TG community is targeted as sexual deviants. It would be a media sensation and most likely news descriptions would range from calling him a crossdresser to a transsexual.

Now let's say a transvestite or crossdresser develops a fetish for wearing revealing clothing and exposing himself in public. Does this mean now that all crossdressers and transvestites are flashers dressing as prostitutes? Of course not, and it certainly does not mean all members of the TG community are either.

It also does not mean that all members of the fetish community are sexual deviants either.

However the same discrimination that runs through other communities, based on the same knee jerk reactions to the same isolated instances, also runs through the fetish community.

I have also, unfortunately, have had to deal with this discrimination as well.

In the world of fetish you have all the same gender identification that you have in any other group. You also meet with the same kind of discrimination. I was under the misguided assumption, much like I was with the music community, that people of the fetish world would be predominantly open minded, accepting people. I was sure that as a member of the fetish community I would be able to feel safe and be myself without persecution. This was not the case.

For the most part, people were very open minded and accepting, but I met many "straight" people who were opposed to, and some outright disgusted by, anything TG related.

There were many groups, chatrooms and online

social networks who flat out refused to allow TG people of any kind to participate and posted vulgar, offensive warnings stating this.

I performed the same experiments that I did going "undercover" in the "straight" world in the "straight" fetish chats and met with the same results. People confided in me over and over their true feelings about pretty much everything.

It seems a little disturbing to me how much more prevalent hatred for GLBT people in the fetish world appears to be than in the regular world. Far more people of the fetish community expressed their hatred of TG people than just ordinary everyday people. Thinking on this now I have a theory why that is. I think it may be because of a more direct intrusion into their sexual world. Like you are walking in on two people having sex and violating the sanctity of their engagement. It may seem to them like a more direct threat to their heterosexuality than it would if you met them on the street where they are not naked and aroused.

As my popularity and my fan-base increased and I became more and more of an icon to the pantyhose , nylon and leg fetish community I was personally discriminated against less and less. I joined a few pantyhose fetish social networks and a number of TG social networks and my videos were viewed by millions of fans over the years world wide. More and more fetishists and TG people talked to me and asked me for advice on everything from "passing in public" to make-up, to "tucking", to dating, to sex, to purchasing clothing.

I was by no means a huge mainstream media celebrity but I was extremely popular on the world wide web and was interviewed and featured in dozens of online magazines, internet radio shows, etc. I reached a level where I could bring heavy traffic to a website, radio show or social network simply by joining and recommending it to my fans and followers. This was why when I did join these networks they were afraid to discriminate against me.

One pantyhose fetish social network in particular, owned and operated by a very popular genetic female pantyhose fetish icon (who shall remain nameless) was thrilled when I joined and brought tons of traffic and new members. Prior to starting this social network the owner had had limited interaction with her fan-base. She spent a great deal of time promoting the new social network to her website fans encouraging them to join. It was free and the member numbers climbed rapidly.

I personally had known who she was for years before actually being befriended by her online and she was a hot topic among many of my fans and people I met in the chatrooms. We shared many of the same fans.

Her new pantyhose fetish social network had a chatroom and the members all had profile pages much like MySpace or Facebook.

Soon, however she started showing her true colors and began talking about complaints from other members about crossdressers posting their pictures on their profiles. It seemed that the "straight" members felt uncomfortable (according to her) socializing with the crossdressers and other TG people on the network. I took my own consensus and could not find a single person to corroborate this. Pretty much *all* of the straight people in the network were on my friends list, they all loved me and not one seemed to have the slightest problem with anyone of *any* gender.

Soon after this new rules were posted stating that all TG's on the site had to post their gender as "male" as well as other restrictions like discouraging straight men who liked wearing pantyhose from posting pictures or joining. She even went so far as to make declarations about how the site was intended for straight men and women who admired pantyhose on women and not for men who actually liked wearing them. Membership numbers plummeted immediately as did her picture and video sales.

I was furious and immediately confronted her about it and received the standard "Oh, I don't mean *you!*" backpedaling response. She didn't mean me because I was *somebody* and she didn't want to piss me off. This just infuriated me. If I was just another average, everyday, person and not a member of the cheer-leading squad or one of the cool kids then she would've given me the boot too.

Apparently, to her great dismay, she came to the realization that the overwhelming majority of her fan-base was not what she had expected. She found out the hard way that most of her fans were crossdressers, transvestites and men who loved wearing and having sex in pantyhose.

Not long after all this the site shut down, she disappeared from the internet and I haven't heard a word from her since. I think that was about nine years ago.

No matter what kind of fan based business you are in; porn, music, movies, writing, you should know who your fans are and accept that without them, like them or not, you are nothing. I have always tried to treat my fans right and have tried to get to know and interact with them as much as possible. It saddens me now that the internet has changed so much since then and limited my ability to communicate with them. I used to be able to interact with literally thousands of fans every week. Now I am lucky if I can communicate with ten to twenty people a week online.

This same kind of thing happens in the Bondage and Domination world as well. I am almost afraid to touch on the B&D world because of all the "experts" and "authorities" on the subject. I'm sure any of them who read this will go on a rampage screaming about all technical discrepancies, etc. I have personally encountered more discrimination, obsession and general "assholedom" in the B&D community than anywhere else.

Now I am not down on the entire B&D lifestyle or community as a whole and there are some great, fun, open minded people in it. I don't want you, the reader, to think that I am biased and attacking this entire group as a whole. As I have repeatedly pointed out, I believe that is the wrong stance to take with any group. I am simply describing my experiences in person and online with many members of this particular group.

I first got into the whole B&D (never S&M – Sadism and Masochism) "scene" years ago when a TG oriented club that I was a regular at started having "Fetish Night" once a week. At this particular venue it was true "fetish" night, open not only to the bondage community but the fetish community as well. I have been to many that were labeled as "fetish" nights where they openly and aggressively deterred fetishists, claiming it was for the B&D community only. Ironically, at most of these, it was more S&M than B&D. If you're only going to serve burgers then take down the "hotdogs" sign.

As I had touched on earlier I was curious about the whole bondage scene, was turned on my the magazines, enjoyed it with some sexual partners so I was all excited to attend. I learned right away that I am a dominant person. I am very outgoing and confident. I also however like to get tied up sometimes too. Not for some deep psychological need to be dominated and controlled because I spend all day being the boss t the office. Because sometimes it just fun and a turn on!

I also quickly learned that this scene is overrun with people who are "Doms" - male tense, or "Dommes" -female tense, who are absolute know-it-all , control freaks who *are* "dominant" because they do have a deep-seated psychological need to get back at someone or the world. There are numerous reasons for this I suppose, but my experience has been that they are "Doms/Dommes" for the same reasons bullies are bullies, which is what a lot of them amount to.

I don't think I have ever met a female "Domme" who was *not* a rape victim or the victim of some kind of male abuse, spousal or parental.

Most of the male "Doms" I have encountered were insecure, downtrodden, picked-on-in-school types who weren't "great with the ladies" until they strapped on their leathers and declared themselves "Master" somebody-or-other. Most "Doms" don't mix well. Putting two of them in the same room is like putting two of those foofy-looking Beta "fighting" fish in the same bowl.

The submissives or "subs" are usually people who enjoy being dominated, some out of a psychological need, others just for fun. I have met many that were just looking for some innocent fun who then ended up getting badly hurt because their

"Master" or "Mistress" went nuts on them.

You have to be very, very careful who you get involved with in this scene many people in it are very unstable. I have seen a lot of people get hurt and I have spent many hours at hospitals and talking to the police when things went wrong for "subs" that I've known.

I have personally witnessed women, men and TG people whipped bloody and driven to the emergency room (so the police wouldn't be involved) while their "Master" tells everyone they are OK they enjoyed it. Then weeks later hearing that the relationship broke up because the sub had had enough. Sound familiar? Maybe like an abusive relationship where the wife finally has enough and leaves the abusive husband?

Back to the point and my personal experience with the B&D community and how it relates to TG people.

I mastered the bullwhip (up to twelve feet) by the time I was about twelve or thirteen years old. I saw one in a gift-shop in Vermont, I think, when I was about nine years old and just had to have it. I think I cost me about $12 of my allowance and gave my mother a conniption fit. I whipped the hell out of my back, my ass, and the backs of my head and legs until I got the hang of it then practiced with it everyday for at least two years before it fell apart and I bought the next one.

By the time I was around thirteen I could do

anything with it. I could whip cigarettes out of people's mouths, snatch things from people's hands, kick someone's ass with it, climb trees, you name it. This was all completely independent of sex, gender identity or the B&D world. It was actually more associated with my interest in martial arts. Until I entered the B&D world. A dominant shemale who actually had mastered the bullwhip. This caused a lot of drooling and a *lot* of petty jealousy.

I ended up doing bullwhip demonstrations every week at the fetish night and started getting people who either wanted me to whip them or wanted me to whip their subs. I told them no until I had a chance to modify one of my whips with a soft leather fall, or thong on the end so that it wouldn't slice flesh. Then, because I knew what I was doing I could whip someone with it causing just the right amount of pain without actually hurting them. Which is the point of safe, fun B&D play. Even at about half the power in the swing, the energy delivered when the whip reaches its target can be brutal. I know exactly how much power to use and can maintain the same control as simply spanking someone with my bare hand. This is not something a novice can learn over night nor is it anywhere near the same thing as using a flogger or a paddle.

I'm sure there are "experts" and "authorities" out there who will contradict that statement, but I am a *real* authority in weaponry, bullwhips, fighting, pain and safety in the *real* world. So to those people I say go screw yourselves and shut up before you get someone else hurt with your ignorance!

I, unfortunately, made the mistake one night of letting the crossdessing host/bar owner use one of my whips as a "prop" during a "session" he performed on he and his wife's "slave" onstage one night. About five minutes into his humiliation and beating of this male "slave" who was shackled to a large wooden cross, the owner who was drunk and later I was told, on cocaine, unhooked my whip from his belt and began savagely beating him.

Myself and several others rushed to the stage to stop him. His inability to use the whip caused it to tangle and he dropped it but not before getting in several good hits that drew blood.

He then tore into his "slave" with a cat o'nine tails type flogger that was way too real fro what he was doing with it and we had to pull him off. He was in a rage and obviously (to me, in my opinion anyway) unstable. The "slave" went into shock and someone rushed him to the emergency room in the back of a car.

That was the last time I was ever there. I just went to play, socialize and have harmless fun. Too many other people were there to get back at I don't know what!

This incident aside, I attended many fetish nights there and later at other bars and clubs before I stopped going altogether. Over this period of time I experienced the discrimination and bigotry that I mentioned earlier.

I ran into many males and females who didn't like TG people showing up at the fetish nights and getting involved. These nights were almost exclusively held in gay bars and were always advertised as open to everyone.

One night in particular was shut down due to a lack of attendance. The lack of attendance was due to boycotting by the "straight" people because they didn't want TG people attending. This was also in a GLBT bar which had regular drag shows and was frequented by members of the TG community including myself. That's kind of like going into a country bar and bitching that you don't want any cowboys there! Only difference is the cowboys would probably throw your bitchy little ass through the window.

This boycott happened about fifteen years ago or more. About two years ago pretty much the exact same thing happened at one of the GLBT clubs that I frequent today. The "straight" people came in with their fetish night and actually had the nerve to say to the owner (who is gay) that it was "getting too gay" and wanted to restrict the gays from coming in on that night. Guess how *that* ended!

I even had members of the B&D community who were supposed to be my friends insist I come to private parties at their houses, then treat me like a social leper when I got there. I would show up and get the looks and whispers that we all get from time to time from the general public. Often I would get badgered with the rude interrogations about my "lifestyle" or my "sex", etc.

I would sometimes be at a fetish night that I regularly attended and get invited to, or hear about, another one someplace else and "friends" would actually have the nerve to tell me, "When you're there don't talk to me, or let anyone know we know each other", because they didn't want other people in the community to know that they socialized with my "kind".

The worst part is when you've been having a relationship with someone involving sex and they tell you they "can't be seen with you".

That actually happened to me recently with a guy I thought was really nice and thought we were going to be friends. After he said that to me I was done with him. I have no time, room or patience in my life for people like that.

The overall point that I was trying to make here is that being a member of the B&D or fetish community also has no bearing on gender identity. These communities or "lifestyles" are populated with people of all genders and all walks of life. So if judges, lawyers, doctors, men, women can all be regarded and accepted by society as "normal" even though they engage in these activities, why should any of use be deemed freaks or outcasts for partaking in the same things? We shouldn't. If these things had anything to do with TG gender identity then *only* TG identifying people would belong to them or be involved in them. If society in general accepts this lifestyle for men and women (to a degree) then TG society should accept TG's who partake to at least the same degree.

I am not talking about the violent, repressed psychopaths and sociopaths, I am talking about the people like me who are in it for the fun and don't get obsessed or over it or do it to the point that it just becomes unacceptable to any sane person.

NINE

It has also been my experience that there are many people out there who associate the TG population strictly with the gay community. There are those who apparently assume that if you have male genitalia and are dressed as a woman that you are gay or that only gay men are attracted to you.

I can't even count how many times a woman has said to me she had a gay "guy friend" that would be "just perfect" for me and would set me up with him.

In my experience gay men are attracted to other *men* and "maleness" so to speak. I don't look like like a masculine man, or behave like one. Most of my friends are gay men and I'm not having sex with or dating any of them. In fact I never have. The activity we engage in the most, next to conversation, is playing pool.

Also in my experience the majority of men who have been attracted to me are attracted to females and or females with male genitalia. There seems to actually be a growing population of males and females who are really only attracted to what I refer to as the "third gender" like myself or TG's in general. Some only to male to female TG's some only to female to male TG's.

The lines of sexual orientation or preference (again depending on your school of thought) appear to be getting more and more blurred. Sexual orientation seems to be taking on a diversity of its own.

I am not a sex therapist or psychoanalyst and I do not claim to know a lot about sexual orientation as it relates to the human populace in general. I can, as I have said, only speak from my own personal experiences and observations.

Many of the men that I have conversed with about this subject either online or in person have insisted that they are heterosexual but find "people like me" sexually attractive. The claim that they could never have sex with a masculine male and the very thought of it turns them off. This whole area gets a bit gray and confusing.

Some men I'm sure are genuine in this sexual preference or orientation but fro how many is it just a kink or a fetish and for how many is it just denial of their homosexuality? More importantly how do you ever really *know* the difference? If someone is lying to themselves bout who they really are then they are lying to you about it as well, even though they may not be doing it intentionally.

For me it's very easy when it comes to my own

identity. I don't lie to myself and never have. I know and can feel who I am, I know what I like and what I want. When it comes to these subjects I am just as honest with people I get involved with as I am with myself.

This is another area where we all end up as equals because when it comes to *any* kind of relationships we all run into the same problems; lying, cheating, self serving agendas, etc.

How often do you hear about or witness men lying to women just to get them into bed or lying to their wives to get something they want? How many times have you heard about men cheating on their wives for extended periods of time? How many times have you heard about women lying to their husbands in the same way?

If you are gay, straight, male, female, or TG you have all the same risks when it comes to this. I have had many, many men hit on me or want to date me while their wives were "out of town". In fact I have heard that probably as many times as I have heard crossdressers say their wives had no idea of their passion for crossdressing.

Some will argue that body language gives away liars or that they simply have a knack or talent for spotting a liar. I am extremely good at telling when people are lying to me and I am actually formally *trained* and educated in it. Still, there is no way for me to *know* what is really going on inside another person's mind. All we can do is make an informed estimate based on our knowledge of that person and hope we come close. We can only make judgments based on a person's *actions* and hope for the best.

I have never been a big fan of marriage as a legally binding contract, as far as I am concerned anyway. I don't judge and I don't preach against legal marriage, but it has always seemed to me like a *legal* marriage in the eyes of the law was taking something as beautiful as love and turning it into a cold, contractual obligation. Why not keep marriage as an expression of love and commitment out of the hands of the law entirely? Let marriage be a spiritual union between two people and their chosen God or religion and keep all of the legal division or union of property and child custody sseparate? For example if two people of any gender want to get married they get married in their church with a ceremony, *then* if each wants their spouse to have joint ownership of all property, joint custody of children, all the current legal privileges that currently come with a legal marriage, they file legal union papers with the state. Make this possible for any two people of any gender, living together or otherwise, over the age of eighteen. That way single people and people with no close relatives or children can designate someone else the same privileges and responsibilities a spouse would have currently without having to be in a long term loving relationship. It seems to me the system we have now is saying that if you do *not* get married and have children or even if you *were* married and your spouse died first *and* you have no other living relatives, then you are required to suffer and die alone, leaving all of your estate to be liquidated by the state.

I have witnessed countless cases of upstanding, heterosexual, church going people going through this and ending up this way. I have had personal acquaintances die alone in the hospital while I was denied visitation because I was not a relative. I have talked to women who weren't allowed to visit or make decisions for lifelong boyfriends as the died simply because they never married. They never married because both partners had been through messy divorces before and were wary of marriage.

This, I believe, would be true separation of church and state as far as the issue of marriage while at the same time still providing all the same privileges currently in place.

I should think that states, mortgage companies, credit companies, hospitals, etc would embrace this. It would reduce the number of people leaving behind debt, unpaid hospital bills, unclaimed property.

There are so many possibilities with this kind of system. People could even dissolve the civil union through a legal process to prevent fraud and then reassign new designees and *stay* married. With the same oppressing government eye regulating the civil unions and division of property that we live under now they could make sure no one was able to abuse the system. Legally the love and the business parts of marriage would be separate but it would still be the same institution.

This is just a basic outline, there would of course be much more legalese involved in the civil union part, but hopefully you get the drift of what I'm saying.

And, since we have freedom of religion in this country already, this would prevent anyone, but your church or religious organization, from infringing on your marital rights.

Again this is just an idea or suggestion. I am not on a political crusade and do not want to be. I do however, believe that any tow consulting adults of any gender, race, creed, religion, etc., should have the right to marry and live together.

I for one do not relish the idea of dying alone with no one to take care of me or visit me in the hospital or make vital decisions on my behalf simply because a bunch of bigoted, ignorant, zealots think it's not OK in *their* specific little *religious* group. Te same system right now is basically saying to heterosexual people that you have to suffer and die alone just because you happened to be unlucky in love.

As I have said, I am not a crusader and this book

is not really intended to make a big political statement or declare right from wrong. It is just an expression of some of my views and the trials and tribulations I have personally faced while just trying to live my life as me.

Getting back to the issue of sexual orientation, I have also had relationships with genetically born women. As I mentioned earlier in the book I dated girls in high school, but I have also had relationships since then with women.

I have never had a relationship with a women who I lied to to about who I was. I met them while I was out being me and they were attracted to me as myself.

This is one way in which I found people of all genders really are the same. Women also behave in all the same ways that men do. They can be just as dishonest with themselves as men can and also just as confused about who they are and what they want.

They can also be ignorant and prejudicial when it comes TG people.

A specific incident that comes to mind was a woman I dated who I had actually known in high school (as a male) then ran into her ten years later as myself. She thought it was so great and our friendship turned into a dating relationship.

She was divorced and now a single mother with a very young daughter. She was also very liberal and boasted endlessly about her open-mindedness. She was also extremely sexually excited by my gender identity.

Not long after our relationship had become a steady thing, however, she abruptly ended it. Her excuse was that she thought I might be dangerous or that I might bring an element of danger around her child because, she said, that she had "known a lot of drag queens" and that "they all carried knives or straight razors, were violent and into drugs...".

She said this to me *after* months of being together where I demonstrated absolutely *no* aggressive, violent or volatile behavior toward her. She knew that I did not do drugs or associate with anyone who did. She knew that I did not drink alcohol. She knew that I worked in the protection field in close association with law enforcement *helping* people. She knew that I did not even do drag shows. I have always had (still to this day) a completely clean criminal record without so much as a minor complaint registered about me. I have never even had a speeding ticket!

I am, as I have explained, *not* a drag queen and I had explained this to her at great length long before she gave me this excuse.

I'm sure some will think that she just wanted to end the relationship for other reasons and used that as an excuse, but I do not believe that is the case. I think she honestly was that ignorant and had what she felt were real concerns born of that ignorance.

She though I was going to be smoking crack and prostituting myself an all the other cliches.

I would certainly like to know what slums she was hanging around in the ten years I didn't see her to find these crack whore drag queens she claimed to have "known". I have never personally known a drag queen that anywhere near resembled that description. In fact I pretty much still know all of the drag queens that I have ever met living around my area and by and large they are very lovely, caring people. I don't know any who carry a straight razor or work street corners, get into fights and smoke crack. That sounds like Hollywood induced paranoia to me.

While there may be drag queens like that out in the real world *somewhere* I am sure that their behavior is not much different from heterosexual males and females from the same area.

When I was doing anti-gang/anti-drug intervention work in high crime/low income neighborhoods in the city I saw plenty of crack addicted prostitutes, drug dealers, gang bangers, etc., and over the course of about ten years only one I encountered was a transvestite or partial crossdresser of some sort and a few were gay men. The overwhelming majority of people engaged in this lifestyle and these types of crimes were heterosexual men and women.

I have *never* encountered a TG street gang bent on violence and dealing drugs. If you say to me,

"Well, then you have never been to the neighborhoods where they are" then I say to you, that just proves my whole point. If TG people are not behaving like lowlifes in the vast majority of neighborhoods that I *have* been to and interacted with them in, but they *are* behaving that way in *other* places, then that behavior is obviously a product of the environment and *not* typical of all TG people everywhere. If this bad behavior was predisposed by gender or gender identity then every TG everywhere would be engaged in such behavior. They are not.

Another aspect of the whole relationship problem is being a *novelty* or simply a fetish to some.

Again I have had personal experience with both women and men being guilty of this. I sometimes have a tendency to play the undercover investigator/survey taker when I am talking to people who are interested in me or trying to "pick me up" in a bar or club. I like to ask them what attracted them to me and some of the replies are astounding and even outright offensive.

I have had people actually say to my face (while trying to get me to go home with them, mind you!) that I am a longtime fetish of theirs, that "you know, it's something different, like doing an Asian chick" (that is a direct quote from an actual interaction!), that they are just curious, that they think it would be a "turn on", or (my personal offensive favorite) "I always wanted to *try it*".

Being regarded as something to just spice things up in the bedroom or as no more than someone's fetish, like rubber or leather or spanking, certainly does nothing for one's self esteem.

This is another aspect of TG life that seems to be grossly distorted by the porn industry. There are thousands, maybe millions, of videos, clips, pictures and erotic stories on the internet about having sex with a TG as a kink or fetish. Often TG people are referred to in these scenarios as "trannies" in a rather objectifying way much like how genetic woman are referred to in them as "whores", "sluts" etc. I personally would like to see that stop. Not the porn, but referring o transsexuals as "trannies". There really is no reason not to refer to them as transsexuals. As I have said before I do not however find the term shemale offensive or derogatory (this is how I often refer to myself) but rather simply descriptive just like, "male" or "female".

Getting back on topic, it seems that many un informed people see these videos online and , once again, using them as a frame of reference, take them to mean that transsexual, transvestites, shemales, crossdresser, etc are simply nothing more than a manufactured fetish or fantasy, like a a woman dressing up in rubber or leather. Like perhaps a man got breast implants and dressed as woman just for the freaky sex thrill of it for the videos. In reality this is not the case. In reality TG's in the porn industry or anywhere else for that matter are simply people of their gender (again like males or females) who happen to be in the porn industry.

I have however met many people who are just simply sexually attracted to my particular gender and found me beautiful or sexy. There are many of those people out there and they are people of all genders, not just males with a kinky fetish.

I have also met many people who were devout heterosexuals who *became attracted* to me after getting to know me as a person. This does actually happen more than one might think, particularly among intellectuals.

I personally find people this open minded very attractive.

TEN

So when it comes to the fight for social acceptance of the TG community it is not about us being a different species or some weird, alien creatures that think differently than other people.

As far as I can tell we *don't* think any differently than males or females of any race. We are all human with all the same thoughts, feelings and problems. We are just another gender that needs to be acknowledged and accepted so that we are not discriminated against on that basis.

Men, women and TG's should all be considered equal in all aspects of life as far as gender is concerned. No one should be discriminated against on the basis of gender. If a person is the best candidate for a particular job then they should get that job regardless of gender or sexual preference. Gender and sexual preference have no bearing whatsoever on the job or job performance.

If a person is not right for a position it should be because they just aren't up to it as a *person* not because of which restroom they have to use!

There is so much sensationalization of everything

in this country today. People get hung up on ridiculous things and blow them way out of proportion simply because everyone else is doing it. If things weren't like this so bad perhaps people would just regard gender as gender. The "straight" men would be attracted to women and have no concern with sexual goings on of GLBT people be cause they would just naturally have no interest in them. "Straight" women would be attracted to men and the sexual goings on of GLBT people would be of no interest to them. Unfortunately this is not the case due to years of making a big deal out of sexual orientation and gender identity all in the name of selling tabloids and boosting ratings. To me this is just as ridiculous as if this had been done to people with different colored eyes. There was actually a time in this country when people were treated as oddballs simply for being left handed! They were referred to as "south paws". I am ambidextrous (can do everything the same with either hand, etc.) and I remember in kindergarten or first grade when the teacher made us determine whether we were left or right handed and actually *told* me that I couldn't be both. I also remember how the other kids made fun of the one kid who was left handed so I used my right. I also noticed how penmanship is completely biased toward right handed people, the letters all even slant to the right which makes the angle difficult for writing with the left hand.

Society is *still* biased against left handed people today. This became very evident to me as I got older and noticed more and more how even though I could use both hands and work from both sides of my body equally, I was forced at every turn to favor the right.

Vehicles are right handed, you shift with your right hand and the accelerator pedal is under your right foot and the ignition is on the right side of the steering wheel.

I also found that when I wanted to buy a left handed guitar, even though, there is no extra cost in manufacturing them, they cost more than a right handed one, simply because society considers left handed people a sort of minority. A *novelty* even.

The point of this is that being left handed is just a product of nature. Left handed people though once thought to be different than "normal" people are now just accepted. Some people are born left handed some right handed. They are not sex fiends, perverts, psychopaths, etc., because they happened to be born left handed. If they are any of those things it is because of some other factors that just as easily and just as commonly affect right handed people.

There has been much in the media lately about allowing TG people to serve in the military also. I do not know much about the inner workings of the military nor do I pretend to know. Nor do I exactly have personal experience with being discriminated against by the military because I suffered serious injuries with long term lasting affects which precluded me from being able to serve when I had intended to while keeping who I was a secret until my term was up. Alas, I never got to enlist so I never had to suffer in silence while I served. I still, however, did get cheated out of serving my country and furthering my career through military service, but for medical reasons, not political or gender related issues.

I *do* however believe (as I stated earlier) that gender should not be an issue. As with any job, if the applicant is physically and psychologically capable of performing the required duties they should be allowed to participate regardless of their gender. If someone pulls you out of a burning helicopter or in some other way saves your life does it *really* matter to you what their gender or sexual orientation is? If you're drowning and a female lifeguard jumps in the water to save you are you going to say "No! Don't touch me! I want that big manly guy back on the beach to come get me! *I think he'll do a better job!*".

As I said I don't know all the reasoning our government and the military have behind the decisions they make about GLBT people serving in the armed forces, you would probably have to talk to someone like Kristin Beck about that or read her books. What I do know is that many other developed countries around the world don't see gender as an issue and do not discriminate against TG people. I have heard that Brazil has third gender public restrooms and allows transgender people to serve in the military just like anyone else.

I imagine that if our nation does allow TG people to serve that there will be some serious reprisals from the overly conservative people and the haters of the world. Also after hearing for years the horror stories about things that have happened to genetic females who have joined the military and fought for their equality, I am concerned about what might lie in store for the first generation or so of TG people who openly enlist.

I have also heard for years the ranting of the overly religious people who wail about how God hates transgender people and it is against God's will and that according to the Bible we shouldn't even be allowed to exist. That our very existence is a sin.

As I mentioned in the first chapter of this book, I was raised in a very Catholic household and I myself am a confirmed Catholic, although I haven't been to church in years. I have my own thoughts and feelings on God and religion that are mine alone and I don't discuss them with anyone. However, being raised a confirmed Catholic I have read the Bible and been formally educated in it and other religions as well. I do not remember any passages in the Bible that directly mention transgenderism of any kind – except in the case of the angels. According to what I have read the angels were either both male and female or neither.

Makes you wonder doesn't it? Maybe we're all angels stuck on Earth and that's why we're the way we are!

But, seriously, these same people who are so religiously dead set against our very existence sometimes like to refer to us as "God's mistakes" practically in the same breaths as when they talk about how God is perfect and infallible. So which is it? Does God make mistakes or is he perfect? Can't have it both ways, and if your God *is* perfect then shouldn't you accept all the people he creates and not judge Him for what you deem are His mistakes? Just from what I have read in the Bible I sure as hell wouldn't want to be any those people standing in front of their God to be judged after calling him a screw up my whole life!

Sadly though, it seems to me that quite a lot of the discrimination and sensationalization surrounding the whole TG/GLBT issues n general come don to superficiality. Appearance. Not just physical appearance per se but also presentation. The way we and our actions are sometimes perceived.

I have overheard people discussing the issues countless times and have lost track of how many times I have heard someone say something like "If they just toned it down a little," or "It's the way they look that bothers me," or "I hate the way they act," or "They all dress like sluts or prostitutes."

It seems that many people think we are aesthetically unpleasing like plastic pink flamingos on the front lawn in a deed restricted neighborhood. That we are "bad for their image" or "bad for the country's image".

I think the people who believe this should take a step back and *really* think about the antics of their precious drug and prostitution addicted Hollywood "straight" celebrities and politicians. Last I heard the United States president that got caught having sex with an intern in the White House was a "straight", *married* man.

I have seen a lot of this bias based on appearance myself, both in person and online. It seems the more "passable" and beautiful a TG is the more socially acceptable it is to people. I have actually been out in public with TG friends who were born more along the physically masculine side and easier to spot has having been born male and seen people make crude remarks to them but not me. I have sen and heard people actually say rude things to others in the group then turn to me and say something like, "...not you though, you look really good you should keep going with it."

Basically they are saying it's only OK for you to be who you are if you *look* what they consider *good.* Like you shouldn't offend their delicate sensibilities with your outward physical appearance by engaging in your little hobby unless you can really pull it off.

It's not a hobby! We're talking about someone's life! Excuse me if my *existence* just doesn't quite pass your oh so importantly art critique!

One aspect of allowing TG people to serve int eh military that does concern me however, is the definition aspect. It seems to me that before the military or the government will pass any kind of bills or rulings, they are going to have to come up with a clear determination of exactly who this action will cover and exactly what will define them.

This could lead to an official legal definition that could cause more harm than good. What if the official ruling is that the military, in addition to gays and lesbians will now allow transgender people to serve? Then they define transgender people as *only* those individuals who are using hormone therapy and gender reassignment surgery to completely change there gender to the opposite gender from which they were born? In this case where does that leave intersexed people and people who simply don't feel the need to have surgery? What about people like me? Just because I happened to be born intersexed and I don't need or want complete gender reassignment surgery I would be left out? This would put me into an even *smaller* minority with *less* of a voice.

I'm not saying that this will happen, but it definitely needs to be considered before a big push is made in the name of the transgender community. These more specific definitions and labels keep driving us all further and further apart and damaging the overall goal which is really equality for *everyone.*

Breaking up into smaller and smaller groups who only accept and fight for their specific ideal keeps driving all of us as a people further and further apart. Instead of all of us coming together as one people with a unified front we are split into tiny squabbling groups who are all out for themselves.

This kind of separation within the TG community really upsets me because I spent years fighting for *all* TG people. I have stuck my neck out for years and fought and talked and tried to change things for the better for the entire TG community as a whole and now, *after* years of fighting for everyone, certain, specific sub-groups within the community discriminate against me. After I fought for them and accepted them and did my part to make headway for *them,* they now suddenly believe it is alright to take that little bit of headway and get for themselves while throwing people like me under the bus.

We really do need to stick together as a community and not split off into elitist little factions all warring with each other about who is really a transsexual or transwoman or who is a crossdresser or who is a transvestite.

I am not one to dictate how other's should dress, behave or represent themselves but It does seem that there are many people out there who are severely tarnishing the overall image of the TG community. There are members of the TG community and pseudo-members, if you will, who are making headlines all the time as a result of their extreme behavior and, as I have explained before, due to the general public's lack of education about us, making us "look bad".

TG's or people misrepresenting themselves as being TG, engaging in prostitution, drug abuse, violence, etc., really do make the rest of us who are just normal, law abiding citizens look bad. Especially when the media is looking for pretty much any opportunity to exploit such behavior in the name of ratings and making a buck.

These kind of people are not going to go away so what we need are people to counteract their negative behavior. We need more upstanding, "normal" TG people to make headlines in a positive manor. We need role models for the younger generations of TG's and for the general public to see that we are not all a bunch of perverts, prostitutes, crack heads, attention seekers and crackpots.

I have tried to be a somewhat decent role model within the TG community but I am no church going saint, nor do I pretend to be. However I have always conducted myself with as much class as possible even when it comes to my adult videos. I have never taken drugs or even portrayed drug use, I don't smoke, I don't drink alcohol and I have never engaged in prostitution no matter how bad my financial situation ever got.

When I go out, which is fairly often, I may dress sexy but I try to do it with class. I do not go out in public dressed like a two dollar whore and have sex with multiple anonymous partners. I certainly do not, nor have I ever, expose myself in public or talk about nothing but sex with everyone I meet.

I was recently looking at the pictures people were posting online from different GLBT Pride events all overt he country and some of them are rather disturbing. There are pictures of TG people holding up signs about TG rights in crowded public places while wearing extremely revealing, "slutty" fetish costumes.

What exactly are we fighting for? The right to be accepted as the gender we identify with or the right to run around in public with our genitals flapping in the wind and acting like sluts? No matter what your gender identity is there is a time and place for everything including sex and fetishism. We are not going to gain positive public opinion with transvestites dressed and acting like Dr. Frank N. Furter running around in public claiming they are fighting for TG rights and equality. Gun rights activists don't gain sympathy when a disturbed young man dresses up in tactical gear and goes on a shooting rampage in a school or movie theater!

As I said, I do not want to tell people how to live and sexual freedom is fine, but there is a proper time and place for it. Like I said before, I used to attend fetish nights at clubs which were designated for such behavior.

Positive role models would go a long way to tip the scales in our favor as far as public opinion is concerned. People like Kristin Beck and Laverne Cox seem to be doing a pretty good job with it. If we could get more TG people like them in the public eye we would make much more headway on the political front. I know there are plenty of TG people out there who are doing good for the community it's just a shame that the media and Hollywood won't give them the exposure we need them to have.

I personally would like to see more TG people represented in a positive manner on broadcast television shows. I would like to see real TG actresses/actors playing TG people working as lawyers, police, business people, etc. on some of these shows instead of the ever stereotypical drug addicted prostitutes, usually played by genetic women or some really overly masculine male actor in an ill fitting dress. It always seems to be one extreme or the other and no realism.

I would also like to see some major motion pictures featuring TG people. There are so many movies being made today about all kinds of "real life" situations and dramas but so few have any serious TG characters in them, even though there are enough of us around to always be in the news! It seems more *unrealistic* not to have a TG character in a movie especially if the movie takes place in a major metropolitan area where there is a higher population of TG people.

I don't want people to feel that this book is a totally negative rant against the world because I feel all TG's are grossly mistreated and I only see the negative in everything. I don't feel that way at all. It's just that equality for the TG community is such an important issue I feel that I need to express just how difficult life really is for may of us. I want to impress on the reader the huge obstacles we face every day through our whole lives that other people may never even encounter.

Imagine something as simple as an everyday trip to the convenience store or supermarket, or perhaps dinner at a restaurant that you (as a "straight" "normal" person) take for granted. You run tot he store or go out to eat, do your thing and come home with no real issues of any kind.

For example, say you go to a local restaurant to eat with your spouse. You wait in line to be seated, the waitresses smile and are friendly, other people in the restaurant, don't even glance up at you as you go to your table or pay any attention while you eat, etc. Sounds about right?

Now, let's say a TG couple goes out for the exact same everyday normal experience. They get out of the car and have to cross the parking lot and hope they don't run into a group of teenagers shouting nasty remarks or even worse a group of adults making threats. They enter the restaurant already feeling self conscious and worried about having a problem. Dozens of people notice them and stare, some smirking and whispering little remarks to each other, some laugh, some shake their heads and make quiet comments about "how wrong that is", some make it a point to be heard saying things out loud like, "that's disgusting".

Pretty much all the eyes in the restaurant follow them to their table. Maybe they will get lucky and the hostess will be nice and seat them with a smile or maybe she will suddenly turn very cold and judgmental because she was brought up to believe what they are "doing" is "wrong".

Then they sit there listening to the constant murmur of snide, disgusted remarks while they eat their dinner hoping the kitchen staff didn't have a good ol' time spitting (or worse) in their food. Maybe they will get lucky and the waitress will be nice and accepting and keep refilling their glasses instead of just disappearing.

Then when it is time to leave the bullies always get a little braver when you are on your way out and they think they'll never see you again so someone will shout something really hateful as

144

they exit the building and pray they make it back to their car without getting jumped and beaten or killed just for being themselves.

Now imagine living pretty much *every* moment of every day like that or worse. Having that constant ostricization *everywhere* you go. To the store, to work, to the beach, to the movies, *everywhere, every day.*

Am I exaggerating? Not at all. How do *I* know this? Because I have been there! Because I have seen it happen to friends. Because I have heard these same stories from hundreds of TG people that I have conversed with.

I have also worked in a restaurant, when I was in high school and personally witnessed, GLBT people being mistreated like this. I have *seen* with my own eyes kitchen staff spit in their food and even saw one of them *masturbate* into their salad the day quit! It disturbs me greatly how naive people can be about life when I hear them say, "Oh things like that don't really go on!".

Well enjoy your salad, but I am very picky about what restaurants I eat in! If I can't watch them make the food, I don't eat there.

The life of the average TG person is not easy and people like to say, "You just have to grin and bear it," or "toughen up.". The people who say these things don't have to deal with it every second of every day. They don't have to worry about getting kicked out their apartments because the landlord doesn't like their "lifestyle", they don't have to worry about getting "fag" spray painted on their cars and the humiliation of people seeing it and/or facing the people at an auto-body shop to have it removed.

Imagine a life where outside of your home you can *never* have a single, *normal* relaxing moment, like a simple dinner out with your spouse or partner, going to the movies, walking in a park, shopping for clothes.

Imagine every time you go out having to worry about going to the bathroom turning into a major project trying to find a unisex restroom so you won't get *arrested* or *killed*.

Imagine having no family to support you because they don't agree with your "lifestyle".

These are just the little everyday problems that many, I would go so far as to say most, of us face. Now add on top of that doctor's visits, hormone therapy, psychological therapy because doctors need to determine if you are *really* who you feel you are before you can get the prescriptions.

What about gender reassignment surgery? How do you pay for it? What if you *can't* and you truly feel you need it to feel complete?

It's no wonder to me at all why so many TG's commit suicide. Life for the everyday, regular person is difficult enough without throwing all this additional stress in on top of it. Then being abandoned by your friends and family because the don't understand doesn't help. Going through all of this personal hell alone can be crushingly depressing. They don't need to be bullied, tormented, abused and ridiculed on top of it.

I am luckier than most I guess, because most of the time I am a very strong, independent person and it seems that I intimidate most people enough to steer clear of me. I guess I am just one of those people that other people can just sense I am no one to mess with. But I believe I am probably an exception to the rule and many others are not so lucky.

I do have my moments though when something will really get to me and make me depressed or make me cry but usually when some hater or just plane ignorant person messes with me I get defensive and sometimes mad and I always stand up for myself. I personally do not believe in always turning the other cheek. It has been my personal experience that when you do it just encourages bullies to keep at it. I've found that with bullies and haters basic dog psychology usually works quite well. If you stand up to them and you really *mean it* they will usually turn tail and run. Especially if you really know how to defend yourself like I do and they get that message.

Another thing that really helps is letting them know you are not afraid to call the police. It seems a lot of the haters and bullies are counting on the fact that TG people out in public are not going to want to involve the police because they are afraid of being "outed" or something. This is not the case with me. I will call 911 on your ass in a heartbeat and have you arrested!

ELEVEN

Hopefully I have talked enough about the negativity that we all face as TG people in a predominantly "straight" society. I wish only to impress upon the reader that not only are we normal people with normal problems just like everyone else but we do also have many more hurdles to face that the average person might never consider.

On the positive side, for me at least, TG life can be just as fulfilling and fun as anyone else's life in big ways and in many little ways.

As I have said, I like to go out with my friends and go to clubs. I love being able to hang out with non judgmental people who truly accept me for who I am and are not just tolerating me or biting their tongues and talking about what a freak I am when they get home as I am sure my brothers and their spouses do.

Like I said before most of my real friends are gay men and we have a lot of fun playing pool and socializing, but I also have some TG friends and many online friends, fans and admirers.

Even though the days of the online chatrooms are pretty much over, I still socialize as much as I can online through the available social networks.

Even though I don't really do any professional modeling any more I still like to take classy pictures from time to time and post them on my Facebook pages. I am still always amazed at the high volume of positive comments I get on my pictures and on my music videos and or songs that I upload.

Music videos are fun to make but there is a lot of work that goes into them. Not just the writing, recording, arranging, engineering, mixing and mastering of the music but the actual shooting and editing of the video itself.

I love audio and video engineering and taking the whole creative process to those steps beyond just writing a song. It may not look like much to the average person but it can be pretty involved and time consuming. I have taken up to eighty hours just to edit one three to four minute music video together!

I am also really into photography (strictly digital photography these days) and I enjoy getting candid shots of people out in the clubs and socializing and having fun.

I often shoot a lot of pictures of the drag queens at the local shows. Some of the gowns and costumes they wear are just fantastic and they put a lot of work into their hair and make up for the shows so that they look absolutely fabulous.

As I'm sure I have already mentioned before, I have not had any real problems with any of the drag queens that I know. Recently, during the shows, they have really been advocating GLBT rights and transgender rights and trying to raise awareness. Usually at some point in every show one of them will make a long speech about TG rights and issues and remind people what a serious topic it is and to get involved. So contrary to what may be going on in Hollywood and on television and the internet, drag queens are not all evil TG haters.

I have also had some positive experiences lately online with other members of the TG community. I have been speaking with many TG people from around the globe and trying to show my support for their different projects.

I have chatted with Kristin Beck online a few times about her fight to gain equality for TG people in the nation and in the armed forces.

I have also chatted with a few TG people about film projects they have been working on to raise awareness through the various film festivals that they can release them in.

Hopefully one day soon films about and featuring TG people will be released in the mainstream theaters around the country.

It is good to know however that there are so

many people in the TG community who are out there doing positive things and fighting for our equality. I like to think that the number of people behaving positively and working toward a common goal is starting to far outweigh the number of people who are segregating and only out for themselves.

There has been a lot of bustle in the news lately about the whole TG rights issue and it's good to see that there are actually some people out there on our side with a lot of exposure who are getting o the talk shows and making waves with the politicians.

It would be greater still if Hollywood would get more wholeheartedly behind the TG rights movement and really push it through the media. It seems these days when Hollywood makes something a big deal it becomes the new trend and people who otherwise wouldn't care or wouldn't go along right on the bandwagon. I think some really well made mainstream films about TG's and the whole rights movement made by some respected producers with some major stars would make a serious positive impact. Look what Tom Hanks did with the film Philadelphia for the whole AIDS awareness movement.

The same I think would hold true for the music industry. If some big name musicians were to get behind us and do something like the Freddy Mercury Concert For Life or something along those lines it would help a lot too. It just seems like TG rights just isn't a hot enough opportunity for any of them to really get involved. Maybe there just isn't enough money to be made from it.

In the mean time we will just have to take it upon ourselves to fight out own fight and spread awareness wherever and whenever we can. That is one of the main reasons I don't get easily offended and storm off when someone starts asking me questions about who I am or the whole TG world. I try to be patient and educate them and answer their questions. Unless, of course they are just being blatantly offensive to get their kicks, then I tell them off and walk away.

However there really are a lot of people out there who are genuinely curious and know little to nothing about the TG world and what it entails. Unless someone takes the time to explain to them what life is like being TG, most people probably would never even begin to imagine it.

Maybe a television campaign of commercials like the ones about not using racial slurs or calling everything "gay" might help. Come to think of it, *why* isn't there a series of commercials running all the time about accepting and not mistreating young transgender students in our schools? I have seen ads about not mistreating young gays or young minorities but no ad campaigns about not mistreating young TG's.

There should also probably be ads for young TG

people to consult their doctors about hormone replacement therapy and gender reassignment surgery or transgenderism in general. It seems to me that every TG person I have ever met had to go through a grueling ordeal of trying find information about these things with no real help from anyone.

All I know is I had to find my own way from when I was very young and I was extremely lucky as far as avoiding the pitfalls or getting confused and depressed. Not everyone is that lucky and trying to find your way through life as a TG can be a very lonely and difficult road.

Thankfully there are many transgender support groups and networks out there now where young TG people can get answers to some of their questions and get pointed in the right direction. They also can find people to talk to and others like themselves so that they do not feel so alone.

I would like to see more of these TG support groups and centers and much more mainstream promotion of them. An ad campaign on TV for local transgender support groups or hotlines would surely be a big step in the right direction also.

Anyway, I have had my share of negative experiences growing up and living my life as me, but I have also had plenty of positive experiences. I have met many interesting people and made lots of friends. I enjoy being me and have no desire to change who I am to appease anyone or to try to fit in anywhere.

It would be nice to be able to go to a restaurant, movie theater or mall without having to worry about being stared at, discriminated against, heckled or attacked but sometimes I wonder if any of that would *really* change even if we were regarded as equals. Straight males and females of all races still get killed senselessly every day because *someone* hates them for *some* reason.

I think it is just an inherent human trait that many people just hate other people for whatever reason hey can dream up because on some level it makes them feel better about themselves. If it's not about gender, then it's about race. If it's not about race then it's about religion. If it's not about religion then it's about politics.

Equality for TG people would still level the playing field however. I would rather be hated equally for all the same stupid reasons everyone else is hated than just for being a different gender that is considered unacceptable. I think it would be much easier to deal with all the regular hate and discrimination we have to face if we didn't have to also worry about the law not protecting us as equally as men and women.

There is always going to be ignorance and hate, but there doesn't *always* have to be actual laws that prevent us from using the restroom, joining the military, getting gainful employment, etc.

I think that once we are treated as equals under

the law, much of the hate and ignorance will begin to fade. People will start to see that it is not right to mistreat us or treat us as less than equals. When something becomes actual *law* people are forced to take it more to heart and develop more respect for it. It becomes real. The consequences for not taking it seriously become *real.*

If we as a group can stick together and continue to make an impact on our political system then we stand a chance fro true equality and maybe someday true *acceptance*. Then we can feel truly free to enjoy our lives just like everyone else, just the way the founding fathers of our country intended life for us here to be.

It is truly sad that our nation which was based on these core beliefs is now so far behind the countries our ancestors fled to escape such oppression.

I have faith however that in the not too distant future all of these walls will come down and we *will* all be equal in the eyes of the law. We just need to be patient. It would have been wonderful if this had happened years ago so that so many of us had not had to hide who we are through what was supposed to be the best years of our lives, but someone has to be first. Everything has to start somewhere. Hopefully things will be much better for the generations to come.

All I can say is that regardless of the ups and downs, pros and cons I have really enjoyed my life and have had a lot of good times. I like being me and I love life. I don't let anyone or anything get me down or stand in my way. I am me and I make no apologies for this fact. If anyone doesn't like it, oh well, too bad for them. I am not here to make sure everyone else enjoys life or gets what they think they deserve. I am not here to ensure anyone else's happiness or quality of life. It is up to the individual to decide how they are going to live their lives and what kind of person they are going to be regardless of their gender. You can be an accepting, caring person whether you are male, female or TG or you can be a miserable bigot. That choice *is* up to you. But make no mistake, what kind of person you choose to be has nothing to do with what gender you are born into or end up as.

A Note From
The Author

I certainly hope that I have not offended any members of the TG community or of the GLBT community with the terminology that I have used in this writing. That was certainly not my intent. I know that terminology regarding the GLBT community seems to keep evolving at an alarming rate and what is politically correct one day is rendered totally unacceptable the next. As I stated early on in the book, I refer to myself as 'shemale' and I personally do not find this term offensive nor do I intend to stop using it in reference to myself simply because certain people have attached the stigma of the adult industry to it.

That just isn't who I am. I am my own person and I do my own thing. To me there is no point in living if you are going to live life according to what others think you should do or say or how they think you should behave. Last I heard this was a free country.

Hopefully I have impressed upon the reader the

main point that was the intention of this writing: that gender has nothing to do with who you are as a person. Gender should not define you, it should simply be an aspect of who you are and not an overly important one to anyone outside yourself. My gender shouldn't be as important to complete strangers as it is to me.

It is my hope that after reading this people will have greater awareness of just how difficult transgender life can be and how trivial gender differences really should be. It should be of no more concern to the average person that someone is transgender than it is that someone is male or female.

People are people regardless of what gender they are and they are going to continue to do all the things that make us people. We do not love, hate, laugh, cry, walk, breath, swim, climb, drive, run, eat, etc., because of our *gender.* We do these things and more because we are *human.*

For all my friends in Florida,
thank you for being there!
– *Vennessa*